JOURNEY OF WEST AFRICAN TEXTILE TRADITIONS

SEYRAM AGBLEZE

For Alfred

ACKNOWLEDGEMENT

I am grateful to the Thetis Blacker Award panel for the 2019 Award. The Temenos Academy's support for this work has been relentless and my heart goes out to them. I would like to also thank The Batik Guild (UK) for their support as well. I deeply acknowledge all the traditional leaders, griots, craftsmen I encountered on my journey and also everyone who has in any way contributed towards this work. This is a clear stand on the shoulders of giants.

Table of Content

Introduction

CHAPTERS

INTRODUCTION

When I embarked on a trip to northern Ghana to observe their indigo dye pits, I least expected I would get caught up in a wave of euphoria that would take me travelling to other West African cultures to observe the various traditional textiles the region has to offer. On this journey, I discovered the fascinating history and traditions that make up these fabrics. This book allows the reader to explore the cultures of West Africa through their textiles.

African textiles are loved by many but little is known about their history. These textiles have a hypnotic effect; the ability to make a grown man go backpacking on a quest to find out more about their existence. I go on a search for the treasures they hold and the mysteries they unfold. I meet the gatekeepers of these cultures and they come in the form of custodians of tradition, chiefs, griots, craftsmen and traders who are helpful on this journey of enlightenment. They open bags of information and I find out more than I had anticipated finding. Tourists visiting Africa love to return with these fabrics as souvenirs and African textiles are in a real sense a piece of Africa.

This book seeks to give all an introduction to the various West African textile traditions.

1

INDIGO CLOTHS

There is something about this place. I remember hearing stories as a child about horse-riding warriors who came from fallen kingdoms to settle in these parts. This region of Ghana is an area distant from the rest in culture and is several kilometers away. One can see Sudano-Sahelian architectural legacies such as the Larabanga mosque built in the year 1421. It is built in similar style as the Djenne mosque, because it is a region with strong Islamic influence dating centuries ago. There are parts of the interior with an ambience that gives you the feeling that time stood still for a while. For a moment, you get a clear glimpse of how it must have been like in the ancient times when warriors walked here. My guide signals me to his direction, I think I know why, I had told him earlier I wanted to get on the back of a camel. We meet the camel's owner in a conversation with another man who seems to be requesting for something, the camel owner then says something to the camel and it eases itself in response! The other man collects the dung in a bag and gives money in return to the camel's owner. My guide then tells me camel dung is important to spiritualists here because it is an important component of a traditional concoction.

My African textiles journey began in the Northern region of Ghana. It has been a place of deep interest to me for a very long time. I embarked on a West African trip that gave me a deeper understanding and appreciation of African Textiles. I had always wanted to make this journey and it felt like a pilgrimage. It began with a travel to observe traditional fabric dyeing here. Traditional dyeing which has been practised in West Africa for centuries still exists in this region of Ghana, though practised by a few artisans in proportion to the population and size of the region. The traditional indigo dye pits used in this practise are also few now and are getting fewer by the day due to availability of convenient modern dyes and coloured threads. In present-day West Africa, only a few traditional dye pits can still be found operational. But in the past, traditional pits were a major source of dyeing fabrics.

There are different types of fabrics originating from this part of Africa. The elements of arts that run through most of these textiles are usually displayed in large motifs, vibrant colours, traditional images/symbols and patterns.

The purpose of this trip was to observe the traditional pit dyeing method used for indigo cloths specifically Adire cloths and Fugu cloth, which are both done traditionally with the same indigo dyeing method. Northern tribes in Ghana are the main producers of Fugu cloth. In times past, they also used to do indigo cloths just like the Adire cloths from Nigeria on the same scale. In Nigeria, there is a 500-year old communal dye pit in Kano known as the Kofar Mata dye pits. The communal dye pits in Northern Ghana can be located at a small community called Daboya. This is a rural community in Northern Ghana which is the only place in Ghana one can still find the traditional indigo dyeing method in practise.

Though few traditional dye pits can also be found in other parts of the Northern region, they are no longer in use. Fugu cloths from Northern Ghana are popular in Ghana. Aside from the ones produced in Daboya, all others produced from other parts of Northern Ghana are no longer produced with traditional dyeing methods. During my stay, I had the opportunity to fully interact with the traditional indigo dyers and weavers.

I arrived at a neighbouring town around mid-day and was given the option to take a bus or go by canoe to Daboya. I opted for the canoe since crossing by the White Volta River was shorter and besides, it would be my first canoe-ride and I wanted that experience.

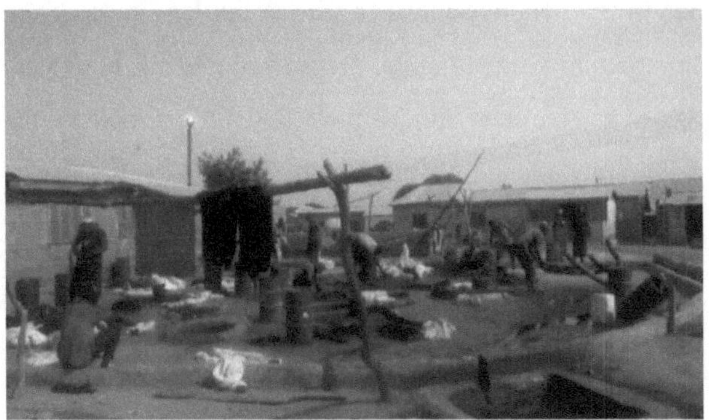

Traditional dye pits in Daboya

Traditional dyeing has a long history in West Africa with first written evidence appearing in the 16th century. There are also examples in Mali dating back to the 11th century, which is coincidentally a country where Sumaila Ndewura Jakpa migrated from. He is the founder of the dynasty of Gonja in Northern Ghana. This was an early 1600 Mande warrior king who settled in parts of Northern Ghana with his tribe by conquering existing tribes on those settlements.

They came along with their craft of dyeing and weaving, according to the oral tradition of surviving generation. Present-day indigenes of Daboya are Gonja by tribe therefore also descendants. These people were accustomed to the type of dyeing done in an earthen pot (pot dyeing) but were later introduced to pit dyeing by Hausas from Nigeria who came to trade. Traditional dye pits here were owned by families but are now generally owned by the community due to intermarriages.

In the past, due to firm Islamic and traditional influences in these parts, the craft of pit dyeing and weaving were strictly profession of men since both sexes were segregated for work and worship. What women mostly did was to pluck the cotton from cotton trees and spin the cotton fibers into threads on spindles. These threads were later hand-woven into cloth by men. Aside from cotton work, women here also designed cloth with simple tools and then dye in pots in their homes (pot dyeing) since pit dyeing was reserved for men. This is similar to Nigeria's Adire cloth which is also done by women. Adire cloth is an indigo dyed Tie and dye fabric made in southern Nigeria. It is popular in the towns of Abeokuta and Ibadan and done by women of the Yoruba tribe. Aside tie and dye techniques, there are other methods used in designing this fabric such as the use of chicken feathers and other tools to draw intricate patterns/motifs. The resist dye techniques used involve the use of palm leaf fibers and cassava paste and dyeing done in indigo dyes. Among the Igbo tribe of Nigeria, one can also find an indigo cloth known as the Ukara cloth.

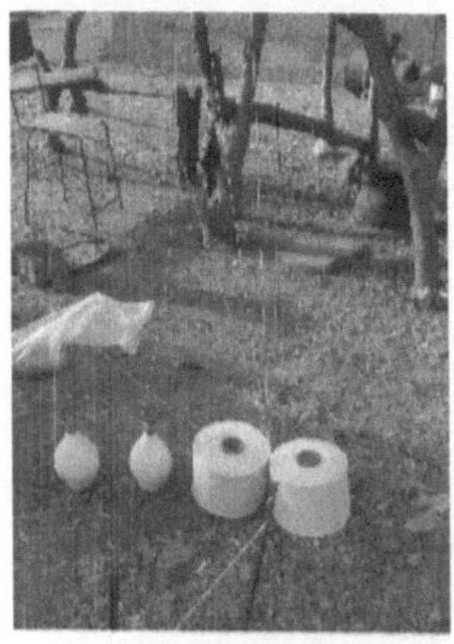

Cotton span to threads (yarn)

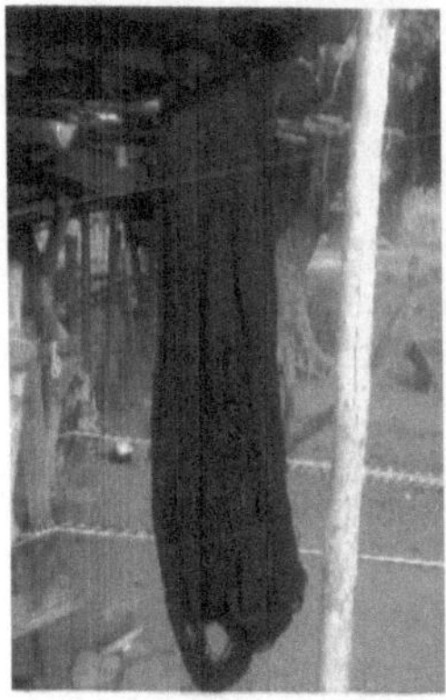

Dyed cotton threads

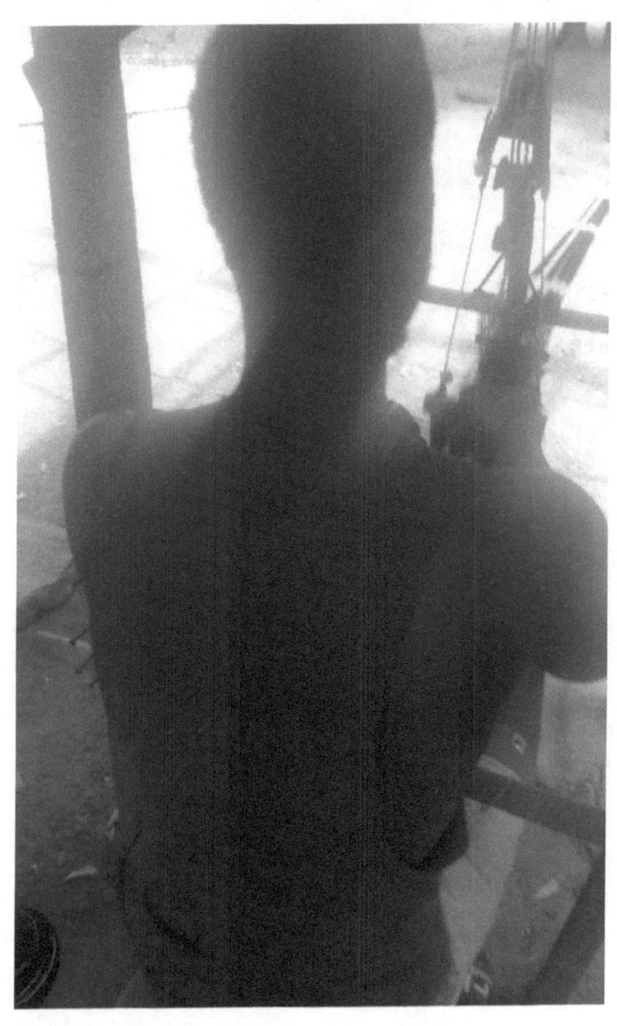

Weaving threads to cloth

In Northern Nigeria, indigo cloths are done by the men, for instance, the ones produced at the Kofar Mata dye pits in Kano. In Daboya too, both strip weaving of cloth and the dyeing as mentioned earlier was reserved for the men. Now the trend here has changed but only a few women join in weaving. They often withdraw when among men during working hours because it is still a male-dominated profession. In Igbo land of Nigeria, it is the opposite since the women rather dominate the weaving of the Akwete cloth which is one of their traditional cloths.

A level of spirituality was attached to making indigo cloth in the past in Daboya, for instance, it was considered a taboo to engage in the craft during night time. Though these were not crimes punishable by physical laws, they were spiritual codes people at the time were conscious of and took serious. An old craftsman I spoke to who still lives by these tenets believes the source of some problems other colleagues face stems out of their disregard of these old ways. However, others, mostly youth believe it to be just superstition. You would also not find a natural cloth used in its original state without dyeing. It is because these types are used as a cloak to wrap dead bodies for burial and it has over time come to represent death here. I have observed during my stay that there are some rural communities in the

Northern region of Ghana that maintain present-day developments and still keep part of their old traditions alive till date.

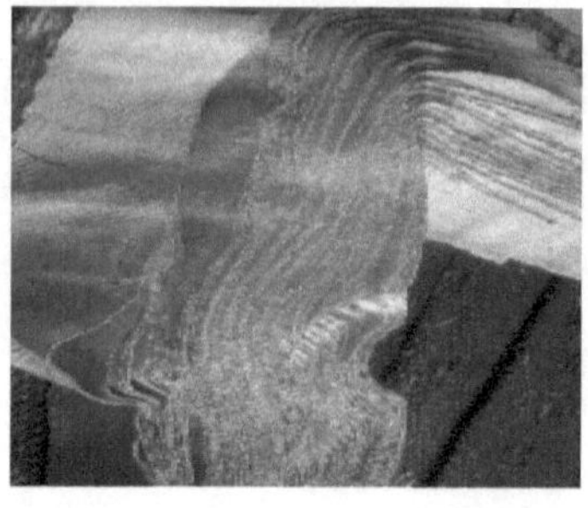

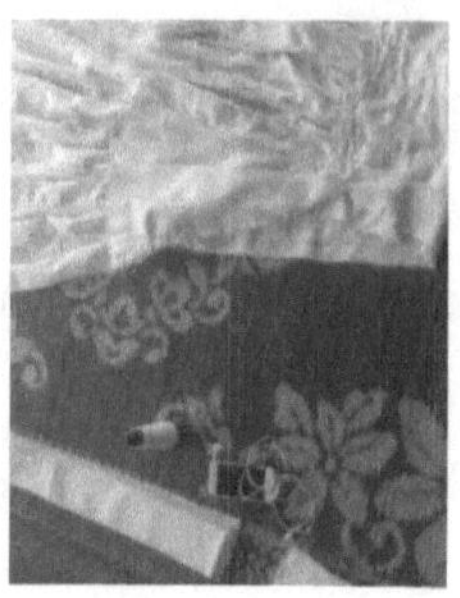

Hand woven stripes
natural cloth

Hand sewing of stripes to

Two types of indigo-dyed cloths were used in Northern Ghana. One which is the usual indigo cloth just as the Adire cloth, Tie-dyes from Nigeria and the other Fugu cloth. The Adire type was made in the past by first weaving span threads from cotton into natural cloth and then stitching or sewing patterns/symbols with threads on the cloth to resist dyes in those parts. After that, the cloth is dyed in the traditional indigo dye bath. Other resist-dye methods of folding, pleating and binding were also used to create beautiful patterns on the cloth. The artisans also used substances such as sap of trees to block the surface of hand-printed patterns before dyeing them into indigo colours.

Other hand-printed versions of this cloth involved one dipping a finger or tool in an indigo dye to draw patterns or designs on the cloth. These indigo fabrics were the popular cloth used by all category of people here in the past but are now rarely produced. When I inquired why, some claimed they are outdated, no longer patronized and have been replaced by contemporary hand-made batiks and machine-printed African wax prints. They also said these particular cloths are more difficult to produce rendering them unprofitable, citing this as the main reason why they are no longer produced on large scale. They are also done by the older women here. I would like to mention that these types of indigo cloth are still popular in Nigeria and Burkina Faso. In present times, weaving of cloth for production is no longer necessary due to available ready-made calico.

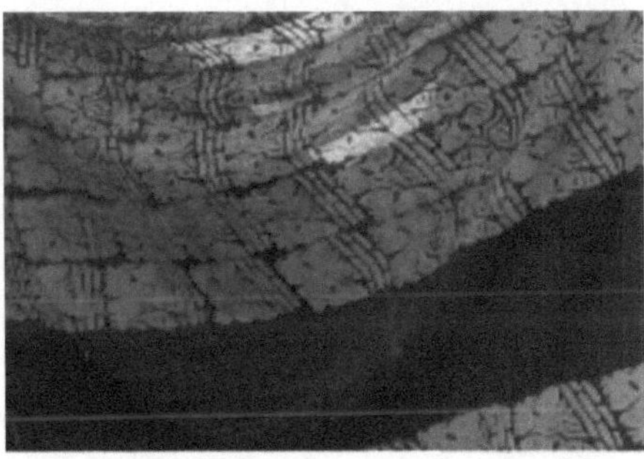

Adire indigo cloth

The other type of indigo cloth which is the indigo-dyed fugu cloth is still being produced on large scale in Northern Ghana, (Daboya). It is well patronized and is more expensive compared to other fabrics on the market. This type is done in reverse, by rather dyeing the yarns/threads to be woven into a cloth first in the indigo dye solution. Parts of the threads are then blocked before dyeing, a technique used to create patterns on the threads to be used for weaving the fugu cloth. In present day, they use inner rubber tubes from lorry (motor) tyres to tie around areas to be blocked, preventing dye there. This rubber then serves as a resist to the indigo dye. Just as the aforementioned indigo cloth, threads and tree sap were also used to serve as a resist to dye for this type as well in times past. As can be seen in the next picture, one can also choose to add other supporting colours which also have to be blocked first before dyeing in indigo solution. Doing this would make those other colours visible. This results in a variety of colours aside indigo in the cloth, though indigo colours remain dominant. One native I spoke with, who also serves as the custodian of dyeing and weaving in this community said he inherited the practise from his father who also had the knowledge passed down to him from his father. Traditional dye pits here were properties of families but are now generally owned by the community.

This Fugu cloth used to be worn by people of high social standing like kings, princes, council members, wealthy individuals and family heads. It used to be associated with prestige and royalty. Perhaps this might be the reason why the fugu cloth survived here, since old customs and traditions no longer restrict its access, there is high demand for the perceived prestige. Not to mention its distinct appearance and texture which also set it apart from most fabrics on the market. The icing on the cake for some is that, fugu cloth (Ghanaian smock) was worn by Kwame Nkrumah (Ghana's first President) on the declaration of independence.

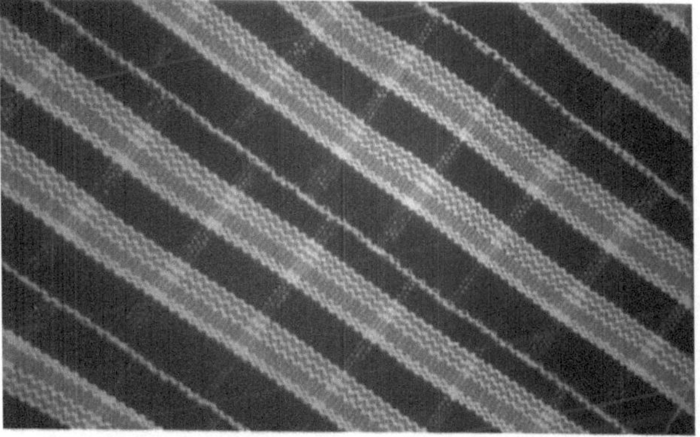

Indigo-dyed fugu cloth

Northern Ghana as a whole has a proud tradition of weaving fugu cloth and sewing the traditional smock. The people here can boast of generations of weavers who transfer craft to the next generation. There were Mossis from Burkina Faso, West Africa who settled in this region. This group also came with their art of weaving and even the word "Fugu" is a Mossi language meaning cloth.

The indigo plant is indeed a gift to man. I have been informed the uses of this plant are many. My new guide cherishes this plant so much that I fear there is even more information that he might be withholding from me. I am more suspicious when they speak to each other in their native language when I ask some questions. After the experience with the camel, I am beginning to open up to any other possibility here. There are different species of the indigo plant, just to mention a few, we have the Indigofera heterantha, Indigofera tinctoria, Indigo arrecta among others. It is possible there are some unknown species too. Some uses of the plant range from dyeing, ornamental and medicinal value. There are however some species said to be dangerous for consumption. Indigo plants are native to this area and have been cultivated for centuries for mostly dyeing purposes. Cotton too has been cultivated here as well. The need arose to grow more when demand was high.

West Africa is among the largest cotton producers in the world, it does well here because the plant feeds on sunshine. During my stay, I wanted to see all these plants with my own eyes and not just hear about them. When I informed my guide, he was hesitant because that meant us changing an earlier arrangement made. I got to know these plants were decreasing rapidly and were no longer in abundance as they were in the past here. Therefore to see the indigo plant meant travelling on a motorbike for about 15 minutes to the closest location. The most convenient mode of transport in this area is by using a motorbike. There was a cotton farm just nearby and we went to have a look. We later arranged for transport to the other village where the indigo plant was and embarked on a forest expedition. It dawned on me minutes later in the forest that I was in the wrong attire. It took some more minutes of walking to locate the indigo plant and it was worth it. I needed to take a picture so I can later verify from experts what species they were.

Traditional indigo dyeing is done here with an indigo plant known in scientific terms as *Lonchocarpus Cyanescens*. This plant serves as a source of dark blue, light blue, blue and black colours which are dominant colours of indigo cloths. As I mentioned earlier, there are other colours used at times to support the indigo colours of indigo cloths. Some other tribes in West Africa prefer other colours mainly for their ceremonial clothes, for instance, the Adinkra cloth by Akans, and those colours also undergo different traditional process of extraction.

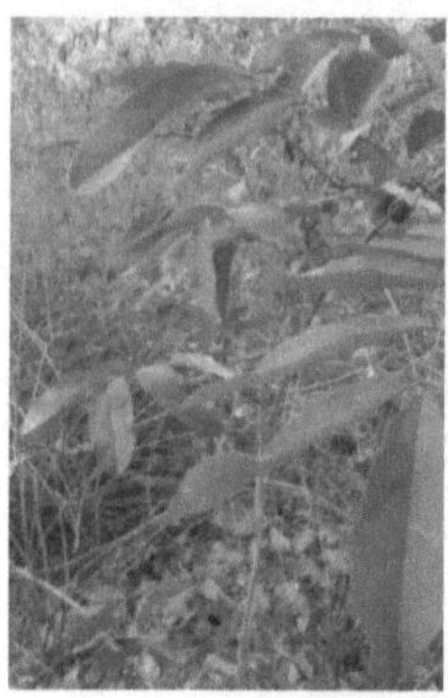

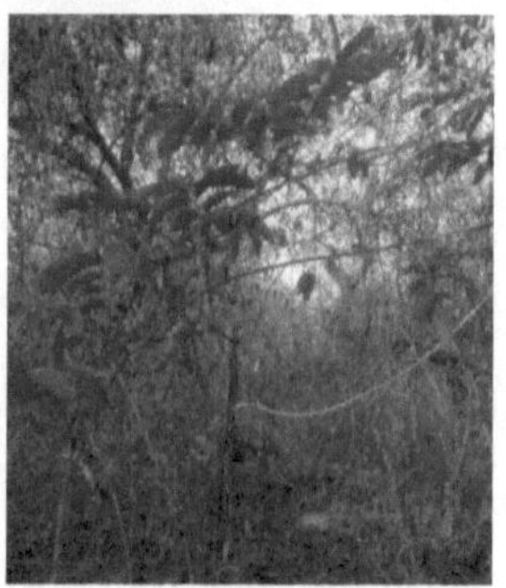

Indigo Plants in Northern Ghana

To begin the indigo dyeing process, one has to get fresh leaves from the indigo plant which are then pounded and moulded into a handful ball. This is then left to dry. After, water is poured on it which should be left for a minimum of one day. It is then transferred into a basket so the water can sieve out totally. You then have your processed indigo leaves to be used for dyeing. This processed indigo leaves can be bought at the market in Northern Ghana from traders who specialize in its preparation. The next thing the dyer needs to prepare is the special ash, which is known here as Zatar. It is prepared here by burning dried indigo leaves and sticks till you get ash. Not any type of wood is used for the burning but particular ones, for instance, one commonly used here is the Dawadawa wood (*Parkia biglobosa*). I have been informed the wood ash contains properties which also helps the zatar serve as mordant in the indigo dye solution. This zatar is normally reused after the indigo dyeing process. It forms a muddy residue at the bottom of the indigo solution in the pit. This is collected and moulded into balls with the leftover dye solution. For the next dyeing session, they are left to dry and burnt overnight with Dawadawa wood for the ash. After the processed indigo leaves and zatar are in place, the dyers proceed to the dyeing pit. Traditional dye pits in Daboya can be found ranging in depths, some as deep as 12 feet. They begin the dyeing process by filling the pit with fresh water to about three-fourths (¾). They then add buckets of zatar to the water in the pit, measuring the number of buckets to the depth of pit in feet. That is to say, 6 buckets of zatar (special ash) should go in a 6 feet pit. As they pour the ash into the water, they pound concurrently with a stick to mash any solid residue so to have a uniform solution in the pit. Thereafter, half-sack of processed indigo leaves is poured into the solution and pounding repeated. They then stir and leave the indigo solution overnight. The next day, they add half-sack of raw dried indigo leaves (unprocessed) to the overnight solution and leave it for another day. The following day, the remaining indigo leaves suspending on the solution are mashed with hands and left for a minimum of 3 days to begin dyeing. I have been also informed the leaves can be left for weeks to ferment in the pit before dyeing begins.

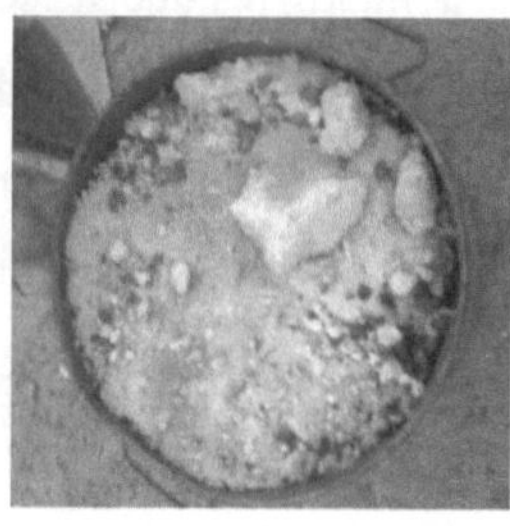

Special ash

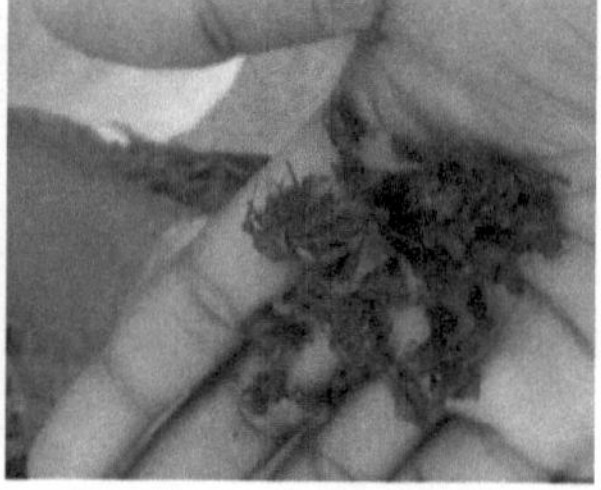

Processed indigo leaves

Before dyeing begins, the fabric is first soaked in water. This is done to relax the texture of the fabric and to make it heavy so it does not suspend on top of the indigo solution.

After it is soaked well enough in water, it is taken out, stretched and water squeezed out. The moist fabric is then dipped into the indigo solution. Please note that the dyer at this point has already blocked parts of the fabric or yarns to resist dye at those portions, in turn, creating patterns of preference. Whiles in the solution for about five minutes, the dyer lifts the cloth out of the solution for air (oxygen) and sunshine in the atmosphere as shown below. This helps bring out the desired shade of colour. This is the reason why traditional dye pits found here in West Africa are without roofs. When first lifted out of the solution, the fabric appears greenish but after oxidizes to indigo.

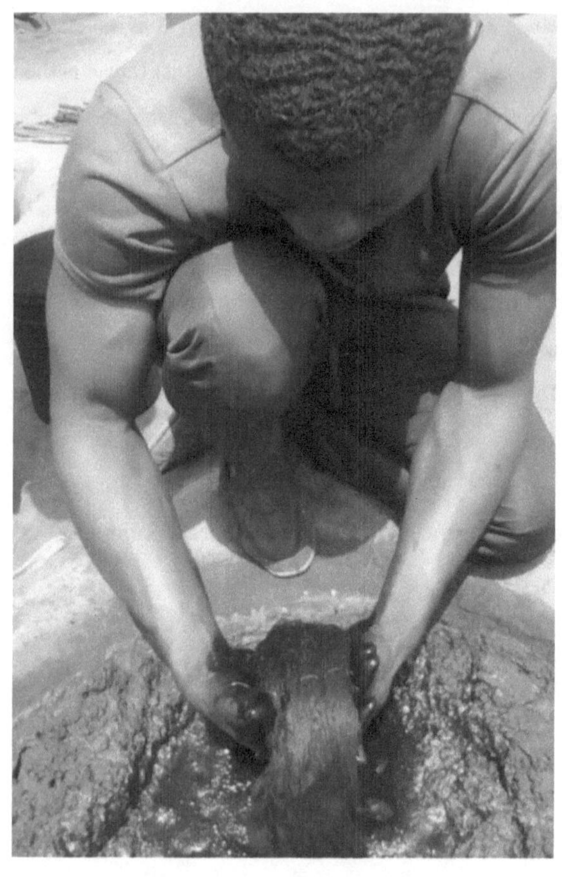

Lifting cloth up for oxygen (N.B Oxidization)

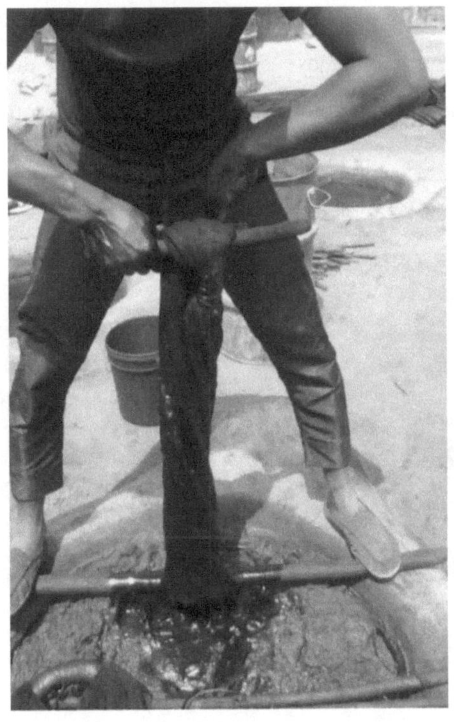

Squeezing out dye for drying

After repeating the dyeing process for some time (30mins and above) based on dyer's preference of colour, the dyer takes out the fabric, squeezes and then dry. Second dyeing is then done to complete the process. The dyers can do as many dyeing as they choose to get the desired shade of colour but in case they want a light blue shade, after first dyeing, they have to wash the fabric in water. The indigo dye solution is considered nontoxic, dyers use bare hands and can be easily identified here with their indigo-stained hands. The remaining dye solution after dyeing fabrics lasts up to a month before losing potency to dye (expires).

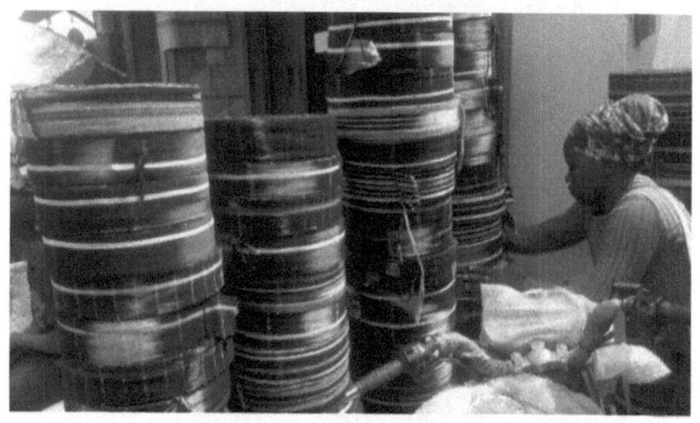

Indigo Fugu cloths at Tamale smock market

Pit indigo dyeing in other parts of West Africa such as Nigeria and Burkina Faso followed the same process of dyeing. There was a flourishing indigo dyeing tradition in Burkina Faso in past times. In the village of Zomkalga for instance, you can find several abandoned dye pits. The Mossis, Berbers , and some other groups in Burkina Faso were very known for indigo dyeing in pits. The Mossis are credited for introducing cultivation of indigo in the past to some parts of the country. The type of indigo plant species cultivated was the Indigofera arrecta referred to in the local language as Gara Zaate. It was mainly cultivated by the women who also specialized in preparing them into balls to be sold to dyers at the market. Aside the family-owned pits in the area, there were communal dye pits which were open to the community. I found out about a system of crafts exchange in Burkina Faso which is also practised in Daboya. By this practise, a craftsman can negotiate to offer his services to another craftsman as payment and vice versa. Take for instance, a weaver who wants a cloth he has woven dyed but does not have the money to pay a dyer can negotiate with the dyer to dye the cloth for him so he would also weave a cloth for the dyer in return. This is an ancient system that some still practise. There is another system where a craftsman can offer his service as dowry payment to his bride's family. I was shown some old abandoned dye pits in Daboya which are said to have been a dowry payment from a Hausa craftsman to a family. Hausa's were the only experts in building dye pits at the time since pot dyeing was what was known to the indigenes of Daboya. This made such a gesture a generous dowry to the family. Owning a dye pit was a source of income. Due to movements and migration by some groups at the time, there was likely exchange of knowledge and expertise in the field of indigo dyeing. I have noticed a chain of hierarchy among dyers despite having a designated leader who is ultimately in charge. This too I am told is steeped in the old tradition. In some other dyeing traditions like that of the Mossi, rituals were performed by the chief dyers when a dye pit was finally completed and unveiled. They did it to attract good fortunes, for instance, in the form of a profitable business. They believe these customs also ward off ill fortunes.

In Daboya, pot dyeing was pushed to the back seat after the introduction of the pit dyeing method. Another contributing factor why it is no longer popular is that, it was only sustained by the older generation of women in making the Adire (Tie and dye) type of cloth. That is why as the making of this particular cloth declined, so did the practise of pot dyeing too. A general procedure requires preparing the solution in a large earthenware pot. This solution contained processed indigo leaves mixed in water with other natural mordants. The cloth is later dyed with the same procedure involved in pit dyeing. Today some artisans who practise pot dyeing elsewhere in Africa integrate the natural dyeing process with other modern methods such as adding caustic soda to the solution. The pot dyeing processes practised in some part of Asia sheds more light on the procedure that might have been followed traditionally here as well. This process involves soaking fresh leaves of indigo plant in water overnight. The next day the plant would ferment into dye and this dye water is sieved from the leaves. Lime is added to the dye water and beaten for several minutes until the colour changes from the original green to a shade of indigo colour. Signifying it has gone through an oxidisation process. This solution is left for 24 hours where the liquid ends up suspending on top of a paste formed below. The liquid is sieved away and the paste later mixed with ash and sugar and left for several days before it is ready to be used for dyeing.

During my stay, I got an idea of a possible way of bringing the old form of fabric making tradition in Daboya with the modern handmade fabric making tradition in West Africa. By looking at how the "old school" old can benefit from the new, in respect to the Adire type of indigo cloth here, so it can be preserved here too as in other West African countries. The modern technique involves transferring or drawing patterns (designs) to a medium block that can be wooden or foam as is now popular with contemporary fabric makers in West Africa. Immersing these blocks (foam or wood) in wax to fix patterns on cloth. The Daboya designs that would have been stitched or hand-printed on cloth can be transferred to any of these medium and used this way. I believe this technique would help reduce the stress and time involved in sewing or hand printing designs as resist done in the past. The design stamped cloths can thereafter be dyed in the traditional dye pits to produce desired cloths. This can help revive a dying breed of indigo cloth here. The Tie-dye versions which require folding and tying do not require this technique since they are relatively simpler to do and do not require sewing designs with thread. I proposed this to some of the dyers because of the reason they gave as mentioned earlier why they no longer produce the Adire type of indigo cloth on large scale. They did not take me serious as I hoped and I understood why. It is a type of fabric they have long moved away from and was done by the older women who are no longer active. This craft was mostly transferred by the mothers to their daughters, but it seems to have stuck with the older generation this time.

The traditional indigo solution is a good source of rich dark blue, blue and black shade which can not be overlooked. Natural dyes also have a way of resonating with artwork. Not long ago, an artist from Cote d'Ivoire experimented with cocoa powder and coffee as dyes for his work and got successful at it. When it comes to fabrics, traditional indigo-dyed fabrics are usually unique in colour and do not fade easily, even for the mere reason they are natural gives them a good placement.

It was a day to my departure and we moved to the market square and had a group meal from the same bowl. The custodian of tradition told me eating from the same bowl is a symbolic gesture in their culture and also signifies trust.

Honestly speaking, I came to Northern Ghana to observe a dying craft but surprised to find the craft very much alive. When I spoke to a 54-year-old native who still does traditional indigo dyeing, I asked him if he thinks modern synthetic dyes and coloured threads might finally replace their traditional indigo dyes too. His response was no, because to him indigo dyeing is an integral part of their culture and has always been their main identity. He went on further to say his father did the craft and his forefathers before him. Now he too does the same craft and has taught his children and grandchildren. He believes their children after them would also inherit it and the cycle would continue. I had the opportunity to also speak with his 16-year-old grandson who is an apprentice at the same time a student. Many people in the rural community of Daboya Northern Ghana, have other occupations but still dye and weave indigo cloths alongside. To these people, it is more than just a means to an end. It is a way of life, part of who they are. A sacred tradition they intend to keep alive.

2

KENTE CLOTH- ASHANTI

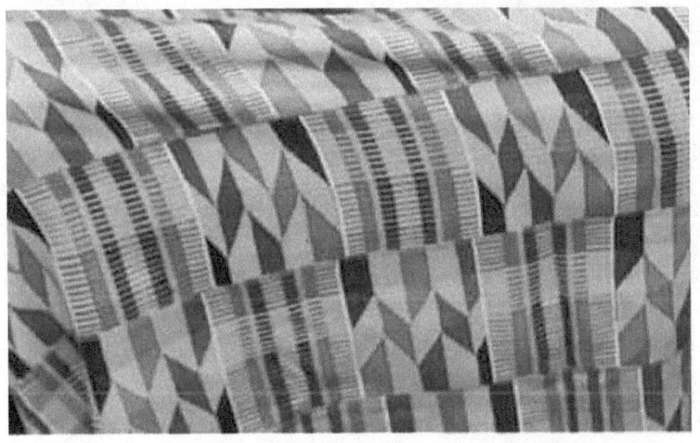

I began the next journey with a trip to Ashanti/Asante. I wanted to know more about the traditional fabrics there. At this point, I was already convinced of the need for an extensive textiles journey and had planned the course to follow. I arrived in Kumasi in the morning and had made plans earlier to meet up with an old friend who had relocated there. We met at the Manhyia palace museum and he was very useful in informing me about the places of interest in the region. I was also introduced to a very reliable driver and guide to take me to my designated routes. I found out places, where I would be visiting for my work were distanced away from the city. I also found out the Ashantis love their king very much.

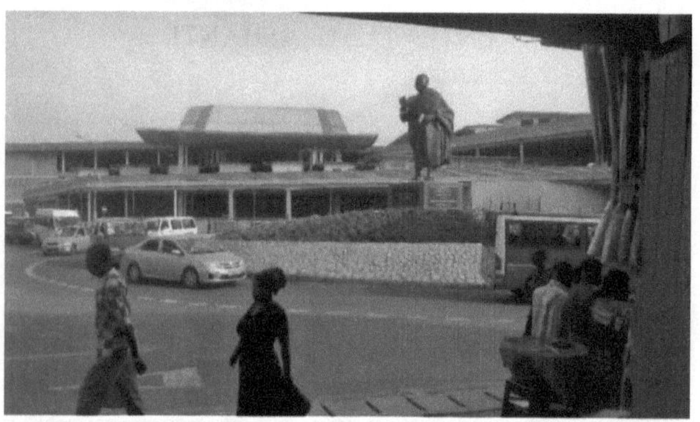

Statue of Ashanti king in Kumasi

The Ashantis belong to the Akan group and refer to their hand-woven cloth as Kente as the Northerners of Ghana refer to theirs as Fugu. Akans are an ethnic group that live predominantly in the West African countries of Ghana and

Ivory Coast/Cote D'Ivoire and speak a Kwa language. There is a longstanding tradition of weaving in this region as well. Bonwire village is the main centre for kente weaving in the Ashanti region. The cloth has a long history in these southern parts. The word Kente means basket in the Akan language which relates to the similarity between weaving the cloth and basket weaving. Kente is a very popular Ghanaian fabric loved for its bright colour patterns and complex designs. It is considered a luxurious cloth worn during festivities, this is why it is more expensive. Kente is made here with the same type of horizontal handloom used in Northern Ghana for making fugu. This handloom is said to be an ancient one. This type is different from the vertical handloom used by Igbo women for weaving Akwete cloth. Archaeological findings revealed weaving devices such as loom and spindles from the ancient Meroitic Empire. Kente is made by weaving narrow strips which are sewn together. The beauty of the cloth depends very much on the weaver. The weaving skills, colour combination and pattern designs he uses all come together to make a great piece of cloth. Anyone visiting Bonwire would be blown away by the beautiful kente fabrics on display at the shops. Professional weavers have their style and can come up with their designs aside from the already known ones. Kente weaving can be very tedious and time-consuming, requiring experience, patience and skill. In choosing colours for kente weaving, the gender of the wearer comes into consideration with the women going for the brighter versions whiles relatively darker versions go for the men. The handloom is operated with both hands and feet when weaving. The feet are used in controlling the handloom. The warp to be used is positioned a distance away from the loom, yet it draws nearer and nearer as more thread is consumed in weaving the cloth. The threads go through a heddle on a shaft and some cords separate the threads so that the weaver can throw the weft through in a rhythm that is a delight to watch when weaving. Silk and cotton threads are mostly used in making kente. The weaving is done by the men here too, it is a respected craft transferred in a family. However, there is also an apprenticeship system in place where people willing to undergo training to become expert weavers go through. I have read of records dating the tradition of weaving in West Africa around the 11th century. An elderly man here who I like to throw my questions to keeps on telling me these are things you cannot accurately put a date on because weaving is as old as the first human civilization. He seems like a knowledgeable man and has some interesting perspectives about the Akan weaving tradition. I have noticed a similar trend in Daboya where older men serve as custodians of tradition and are people with more information about the history and traditions of their communities. They operate as the ancient griots I have heard about. Griots are West African historians who are the custodians of oral traditions of their kingdoms or settlements. It is possibly a contributing factor to the survival of such traditions since these areas are more conservative and entrenched in native culture. I have also noticed that the communities of crafts (weaving, dyeing, fabric making) are lesser developed when comparing them to the other parts of the region where they are located. They are mostly suburbs of urban areas.

Akan oral tradition tells a tale of two friends learning the craft from observing a spider weave its web. The two friends later experimented first with palm leave fibers and then finally cotton which ended up originating kente cloth. In my opinion, to fully grasp this concept, you have to understand that spider stands for knowledge in Ashanti mythology. It is called Ananse in the Akan language. There are several Akan folklore centred on this particular creature. Some even refer to it as a god of knowledge, and I believe it is indeed from a great source of knowledge that one can originate such a complex and skilful craft. This cloth is highly-priced in Akan tradition and has so many patterns that have their meanings and stories. In the past, a selection of kente was even made with golden threads for the king and royal household. There is a traditional way of wearing cloth for both men and women. One's ability to wear the cloth that way says a lot about him or her. You would find fathers teaching their sons who grew up in the cities how to best wear the cloth, since how easy one can wear it is visible evidence of one's maturity and knowledge of his native culture. You would normally see it worn traditionally in a fashion draped across the left shoulder for men and with the women, the cloth is mostly wrapped above the breast region. In new age fashion, you would see variations of this same style in some women dresses here. Kente is also used in the academic sphere by graduating students in Africa and the diaspora. It is a strong cultural identity.

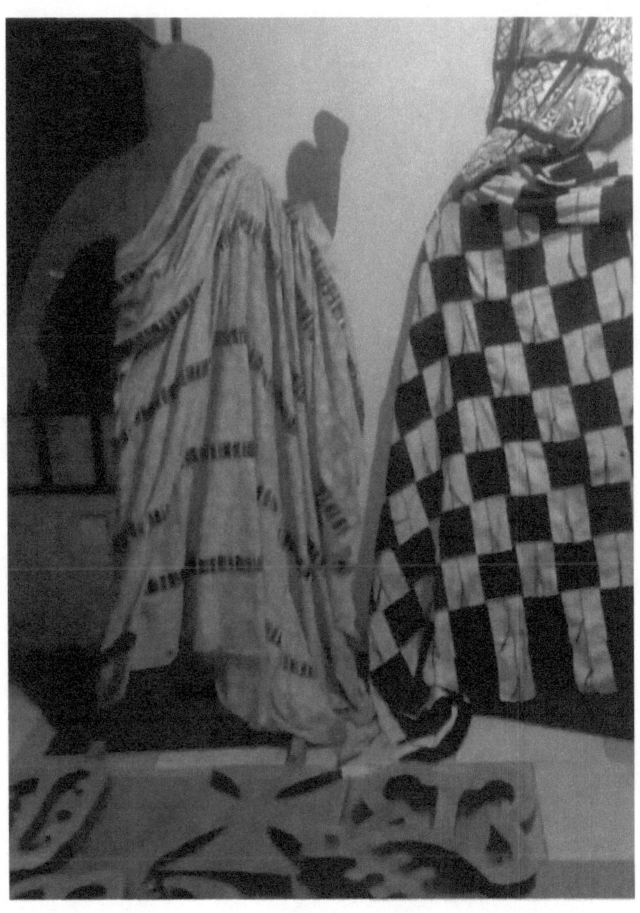

From the image on left you can see the way cloth is worn traditionally by men.

Some Ashanti Kente Patterns with Meanings

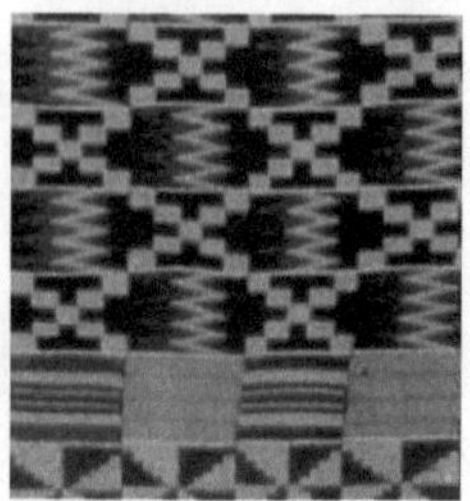

Obaakofo mmu Man: A single individual does not rule a state.

This is a popular notion held in Akan tradition. The knowledge of one person cannot be depended on to always pass the right judgment in every situation. This ideology stresses on the fact that for effective leadership, every ruler, be it a king or chief should not fall into the trap of depending solely on their wisdom to lead. That is why the institution of the council of elders was constituted to assist them in making decisions on behalf of the kingdom. It also serves as a caution against autocracy and abuse of royal power.

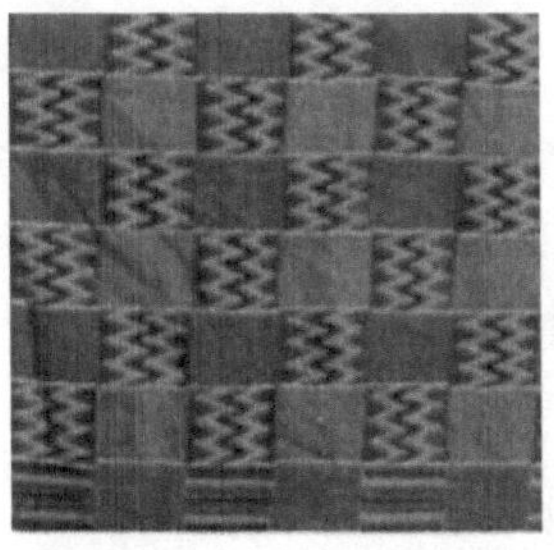

Sika Futuro: Gold dust.

This represents abundance of wealth. In the past, gold dust was a form of currency in the kingdom of Ashanti. Therefore naming this particular pattern after it is a representation of riches and other achievements. It is also a display of royalty.

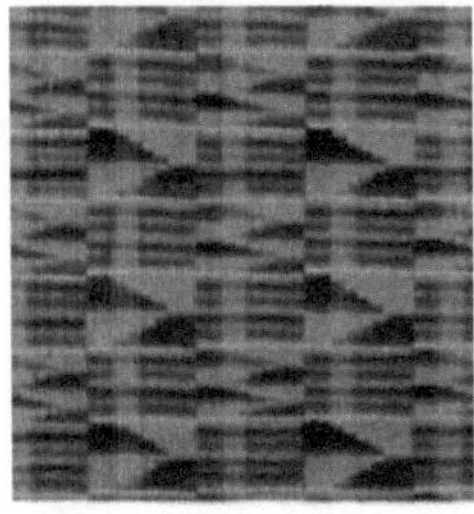

Adwenasa: An exhausted mind

This design represents the highest level of artistry in weaving the kente cloth and therefore considered as a high quality and prestigious pattern among the others. It was said to be originated by one of the best weavers in the past.

He sought to create a masterpiece at the time for the king. One that would be like no other ever produced, it took all his efforts with influences from all motifs at the time, reaching a point where he realized he had exceeded his limit. Having nothing more to add to the design made him conclude the piece, making it his best work. This was one of the exclusive designs worn by the Ashanti king. It is a source of inspiration to people. It entreats us to push ourselves to exceed the limits we set for ourselves, in turn bringing out our very best.

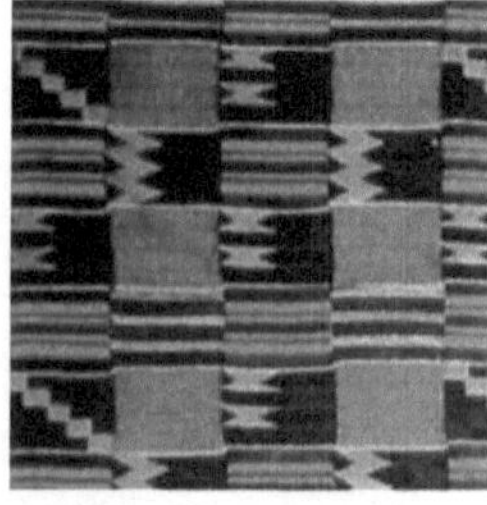

Abusua Ye Dom: Family is a great force.

This design reflects the importance of family in one's life. In Akan culture, the family a person comes from is their protection and pride. It reinforces the bond of a family. The Akans have an interesting family relationship where the extended family members are considered as close as the nuclear family members are.

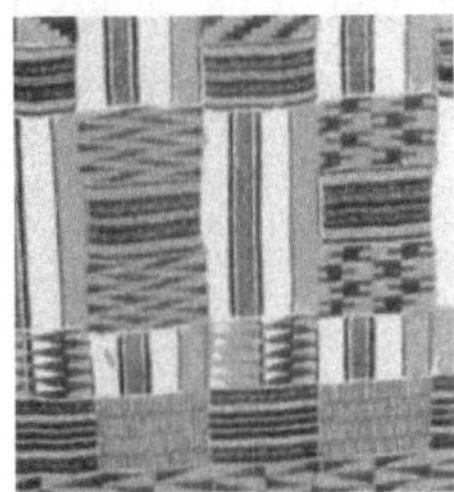

Toku kra Toma: Soul of Toku cloth.

This design was commissioned in honour of a past fallen female warrior for her inspiring courage in a battle fought in the 1700s. She was also a queen mother of the kingdom. The Ashanti kingdom gives special recognition and status to women in their society. This is one reason exploits of women echo throughout their history. Another popular woman in their history is Yaa Asanteewaa. She led the kingdom to war in her time.

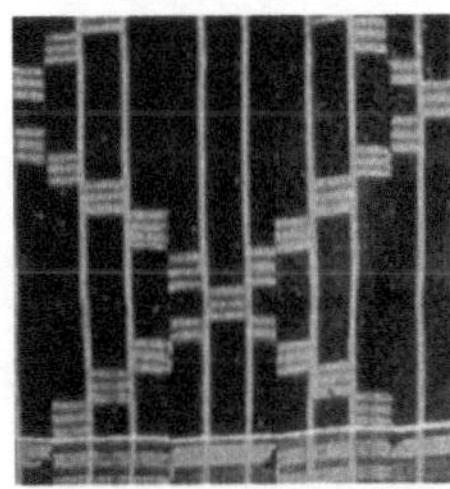

Akempem: Thousands of shields

It represents the security of Ashanti from foreign aggression. In the old days, shields were used by their soldiers on the battlefield and the kingdom had a great military force. This is why shield has come to represent security in the design.

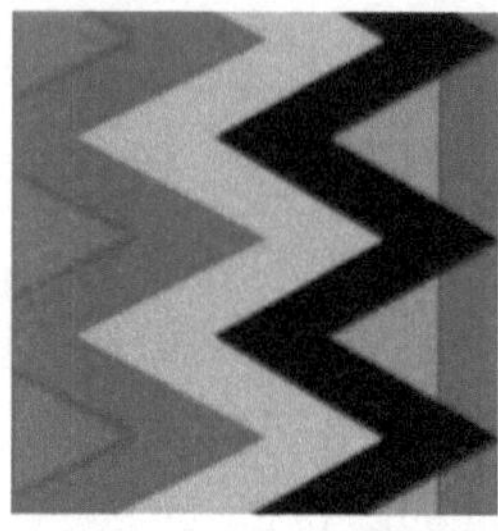

Nkyimkyim: Zig Zag

This pattern reflects the uncertainties of life, which makes it not a smooth journey or a straight path. It cautions one to always be prepared for whatever situation, be it a good one or a bad one and not expecting to always have things go the way they anticipated or planned.

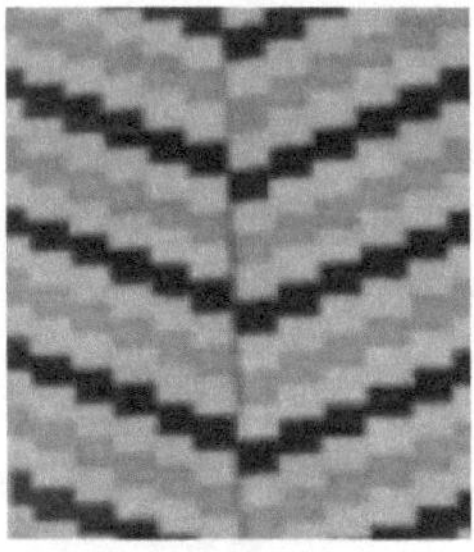

Obi nkye obi kwa mu si: To err is human

This design highlights the need to forgive those who have offended you because it is not in the nature of man to be perfect. Everyone has a bad side thereby the need to tolerate people in general to co-exist with a peace of mind.

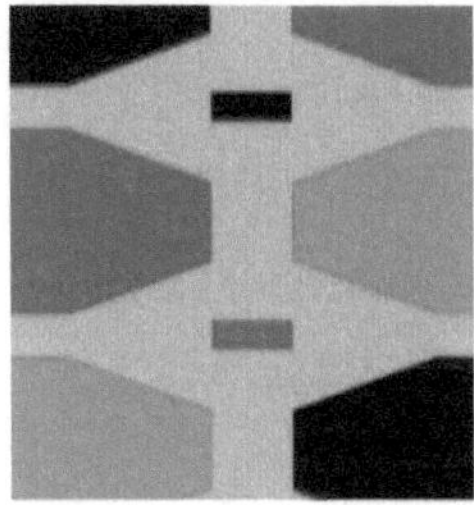

Ohene Anewa: A king sees far

Ohene Anewa is a representation of the influence of the king, seeing everything that goes on in the kingdom and aware of every development. Nothing can be hidden from him because he has to know what pertains to the state. The pattern also reflects his vision for the kingdom.

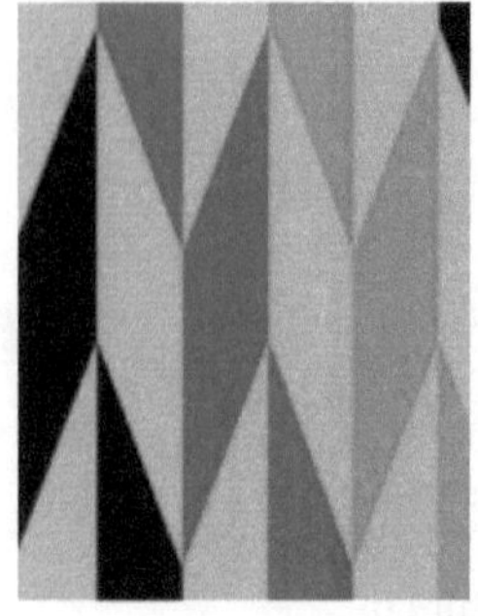

Niata: A two-edged sword

Sword plays a vital role in the culture of the Ashantis. It is used on important ceremonies such as when the monarch is taking his oath-of-office. He holds the sword when making his proclamation and vows to his subjects. It is used by his subordinate chiefs too. It was also used by the leaders of the vassal states and citizens when swearing allegiance to the king. It was one of the popular weapons also used in warfare by the soldiers of the kingdom.

Some say early kente was dominated with mainly blue shades of colour like the fugu cloth before other colours were later added. That is to suggest that indigo dyeing was the most popular dyeing technique at the time, but this theory has not been proven. However, in some Nigerian cultures, you would notice some indigenous fabrics looking just like the fugu cloth in Northern Ghana. Same can be said of some indigenous Beninese textiles, others also resemble kente.

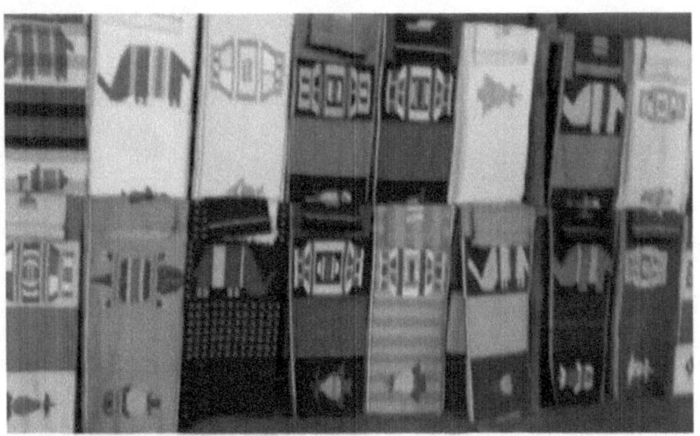

Some hand woven Beninese textile

3

KENTE CLOTH- EWE

The Kente cloth is not only associated with Akans but also with other groups in southern Ghana such as the Ewes. Ewes are part of the Gbe language speakers group. Kente is popular with the Ewe people and means to open and press in the Ewe language, relating to one's movement (rhythm) whiles weaving the cloth. Ewe people also dress in the kente regalia during ceremonies but unlike the Ashantis, they sometimes wear a short sleeve shirt (inner garment) beneath the cloth. One of the main centres of weaving can be found at Agortime Kpetoe and the Ewes of this area celebrate an annual festival called the Agortime Kente Festival. This is to celebrate their kente tradition. They also use it to mark their migration from Notsie, to the current location in Ghana. There is no need to separate these two because there is a notable link between them. They both make up their history. One native of Agortime Kpetoe that I spoke with told me kente tells their story because it was a cloth their forefathers wore when making the journey to their current location. In other words, it is a tradition that came along with them and stayed. During this celebration, they unveil new kente design(s) and give this design(s) a name that stands for something or someone important. In some cases the designs have meanings.

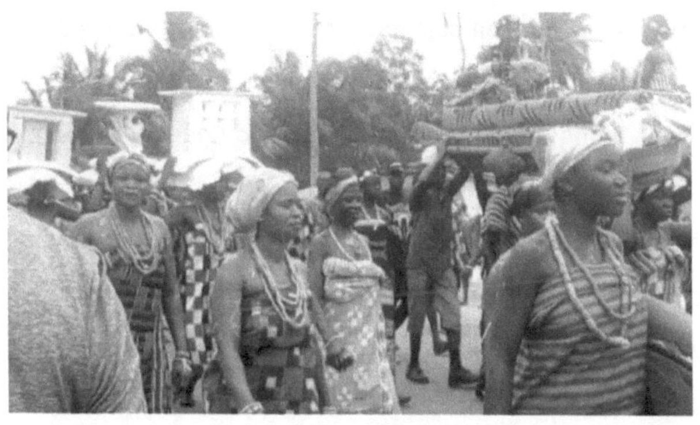

Agortime kente festival. (N.B From the picture one can see an Ewe chief carried in a palanquin and people carrying traditional stools from behind. Also in the picture we can see women wearing varieties of kente cloth traditionally. This is one of the ways it is traditionally worn by women)

Aside from the festival here, there are other known festivals by other Ewe towns that commemorate the migration story. One is the Hogbetsotso festival, Hogbetsotso is an Ewe word that means to uproot and cross over. Which is self-explanatory because they uprooted themselves from where they had considered home and crossed over to an unknown land. This migration took place 400 years ago in an ancient kingdom called Notsie. It was located in present-day Togo and made up of Ewe speakers. Notsie is said to have been an economically stable state and had been a major trading centre around the 16th century. A lively thriving society where citizens lived in peace and had instituted festivals celebrated annually too. On one of their celebrations, a misunderstanding broke out between two elders of different clans in the kingdom. Even though Notsie was a state unified under one rule of a King called Agorkoli, it was made up of different clans who lived in settlements quite apart. The misunderstanding resulted in a fight and because they were elders of different clans, their fellow clansmen present at the celebration ground joined in. This ended up as a group fight. Since they belonged to different clans, it is possible there was prevailing tension between them due to trivial politics. These two groups were the Dogbos (migrating Ewes) and the Notsies. The Notsies were also the clan of the ruling monarch. Unfortunately during the fight, the elder from the Dogbos (Aga by name) got severely injured by a man from the other clan and was rushed away in an unconscious state. This other man was called Dzedua and was also a close relative of the king (Agorkorli). Some historians say he was a nephew of the king. The injured Aga was treated and he later regained consciousness. Not long after this incident, a different elder from the Dogbos died out of natural causes and was not in any way involved in the earlier scuffle that took place on the durbar grounds. But out of mischief, the Dogbos informed the king that it was the elder who was injured in the fight that had died from the injuries sustained. According to prevailing customs of the kingdom, it was ruled as murder and Dzedua was executed for the "crime committed". After the deed was done, the Dogbos sought to conceal what they had done. But it was later revealed by a member of the clan who was heavily drunk at a drinking spot. Oral tradition records that some of the words he uttered were; "We are the ones from Adzatome, avengers of the living". The king later found out and was deeply aggrieved. The Dogbos tried to save the situation by smuggling the elder out of the kingdom. The king got to know of his escape, and sent warriors after him for justice to be served but he was not found. When the king heard they did not find him, he was infuriated and made up his mind to deal with the Dogbos for what they have done. He began by ordering them to build an imposing wall made of earth around the entire kingdom and another around his palace. Aside from this great task, he instructed them to add prickly thorns, piece of rock and broken pots to the mixture of building materials. This was intended to make the task unbearable for them. With toil and sweat, they completed the wall but it did not end there. He went on giving them difficult tasks upon difficult tasks. The king is said to have ordered them on one occasion to capture a lion from a forest. This resulted in some deaths. All the Dogbo youth were conscripted into the king's army and sent on the most dangerous missions simply to get rid of as many as possible. They were oppressed in the kingdom and began to feel like second class citizens in their homeland. They sent a delegation to plead with the king all to no avail. This made them hatch a plan of escape. The best hunters were given the task of scouting for possible new settlements and also discover previously unknown paths to follow on their away journey. This would make it difficult to be traced. The women were advised to empty every wastewater on a particular spot of the wall so that it would become weak overtime for the men to dig a hole through easily. On a rainy season when there had been a persistent rainfall, it was decided to take action. After successfully creating this hole they exited through it at midnight when the Notsie people were fast asleep. The women and children went through first, the elderly followed and the able young men were the last out. They embarked on a journey to a new land. This was a journey of freedom. Remnants of the famous wall of Notsie still stands in present-day Togo.

They moved out of their homeland because of a cruel king. It is believed that this is why the Ewes decided never more to have a central political power (king) that they would submit to as subjects. But rather have heads of clans in place who would not have that much power, in turn operating in a more democratic dispensation. It explains why in the Ewe society one can find numerous chiefs. After settling as separate groups in different parts of south-eastern Ghana, these clans would develop into chiefdoms. But despite maintaining this system, some made military alliances within their member groups who settled on other settlements in the new land. So to count on each other in the future when the need arises. This theory about their system of governance might be the reason why in Ewe tradition, there is no kente made exclusively for the monarch as in the case of Ashanti's kente. Their system is more fashioned towards an egalitarian society. They have a history with autocratic leadership that even predates the Notsie saga. They had migrated from other places before settling at Notsie in the first place. Their history is marked with journeying, away from oppression, persecution and dictatorship. Hence the need to adopt a system to prevent such phenomenon from reoccurring in the future. One Ewe historian by the name Agbotadua Kumassah who is also a traditional leader made the point in his book that in the Ewe monarch system, the monarch operates as a constitutional head. He is more of a ceremonial leader assisted by a council of state made up of elders. These elders are also mostly from the different clans that make up the state and they are actively involved in every decision-making process concerning the state.

There is no major difference in the appearance of the Ewe and Ashanti (Akan) kente. It would be difficult to differentiate between them. They are both done with the same weaving style. The ewe weavers are also mostly men and they use the same horizontal handloom. As I mentioned earlier, what makes the difference in kente is the weaver and by that, I mean his level of skill and experience. One thing that I have noticed about the ewe kente tradition is the existence of some animal motifs as can be seen in the next illustration. Similar to that of the Beninese hand woven textile.

Some Ewe Kente Patterns with Meanings

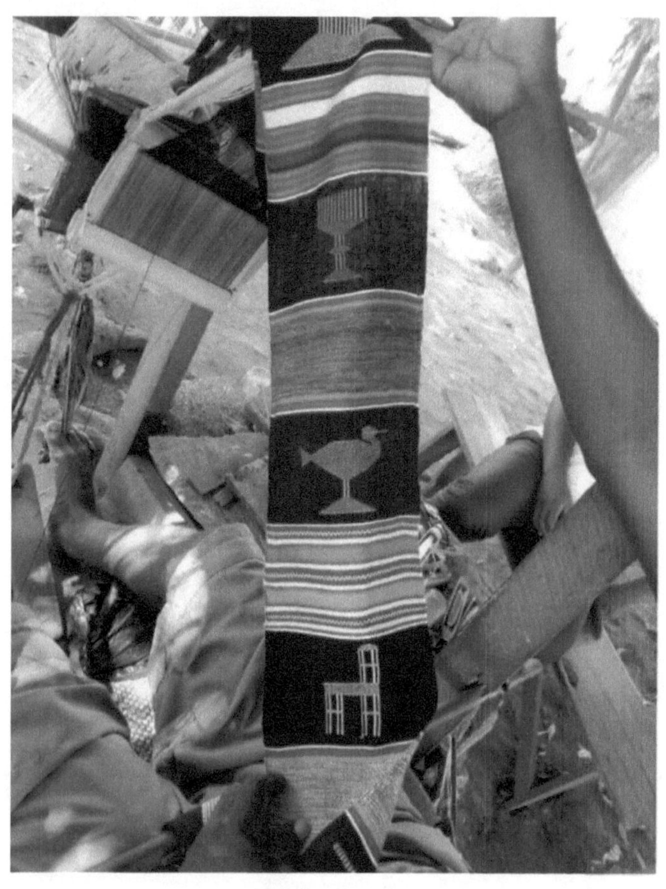

(N.B You would notice the same horizontal type of hand loom used in Northern Ghana)

Xexeame do atsuion : Beauty of the world

The Beauty-of-the-world kente pattern highlights the appreciation of life and nature. Things in life to be grateful for, spanning from the natural wonders around us that are full of beauty, and the need to care and preserve them. It also points out the ingenuity of man displayed through all forms of creativity. The entire design basically talks about the need to embrace life and all the beautiful creations it has to offer. This is one concept in Ewe mythology that stresses on not losing sight of the things that really matter. It advises us to desist from occupying ourselves with trivial things that would make us miss out on the true treasures and joy of life.

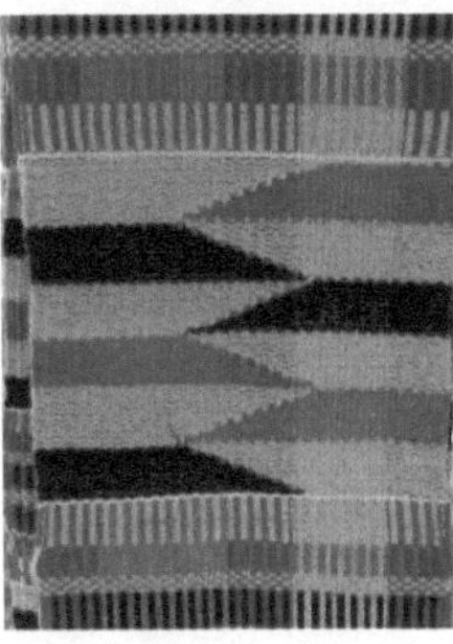

koliko kakae: pieces of sliced yam

This design was named this way because it is said that the shapes look just like the shapes of sliced yam. This name started as an alias for the design but stuck with it. It is an old pattern, one of the original kente designs but the actual name got lost along the way. I was told there are lots of the old designs whose original names have been corrupted or lost over the years and have been given new names.

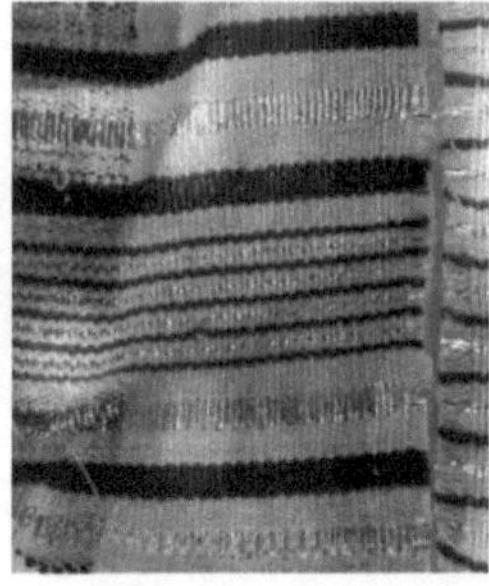

Srordevor : Wedding cloth

As the name suggests this is a pattern used during marriage ceremonies. This stems from the old tradition of dedicating some designs for special events.

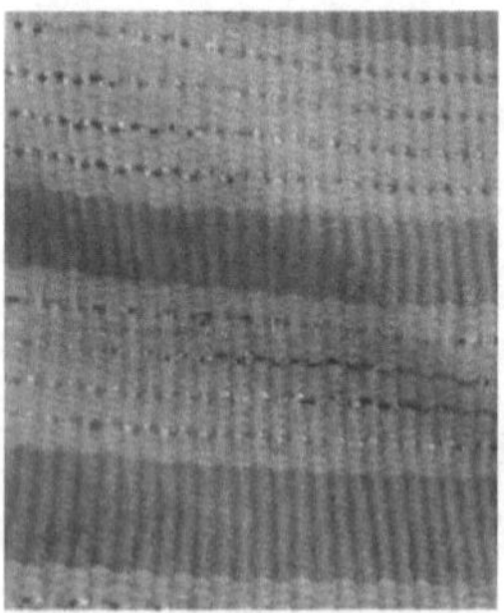

Yesu fe forfor nkeke: Easter Sunday

This falls in the category of modern designs. It has been fused with Christianity. Marking Easter Sunday festivities where most people wear such colours to church. Most Ghanaians are Christians therefore, the need arose for some Ewe weavers in the new tradition to use some Christian influences on their designs. They are many new designs of the Ewe kente that fall under this category.

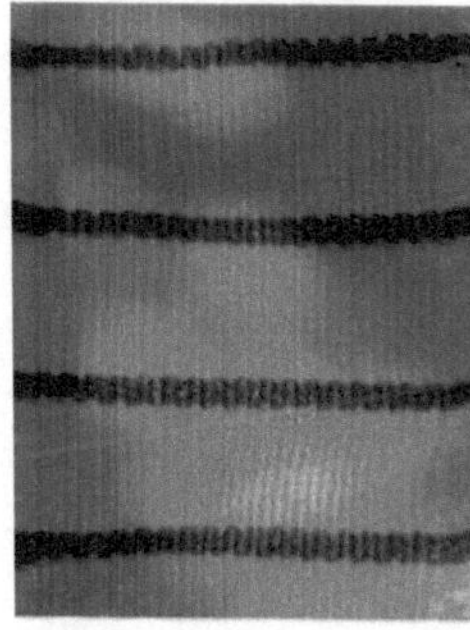

Miator gbekorviwo: Difficult times

This is one of the old designs in the traditional society that represented a state of emergency. This was the pattern for war garments that is why when worn signalled dangerous times. I was also informed it bears a similarity to the traditional hunting garment too.

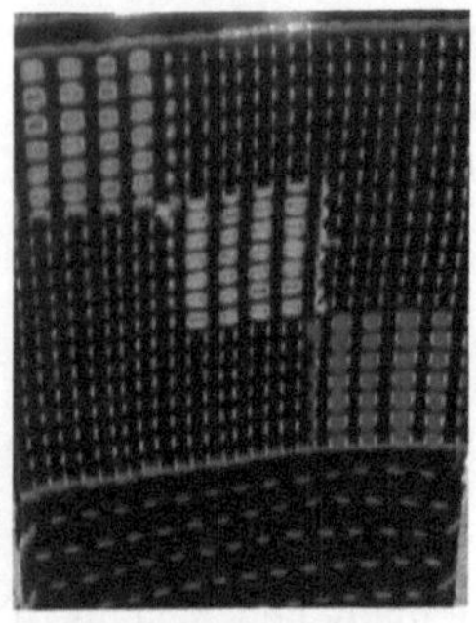

Hiator medua kpe oo: A poor man does not eat stone.

This is a design that encourages people not to look down on themselves even if they think they do not have money or lack in a certain regard. It signifies that things would get better at the right time. And to always have a positive mindset even in a bad situation, because survival is part of man's existence.

4

ADINKRA

Adinkra cloth is also used as a ceremonial cloth in Akan culture. This cloth is made with old Akan ideograms or you can say Akan tribal symbols that carry meaning. The motifs of Adinkra are still relevant to Akans today as they ever were in the past and remain very popular. In present times, most Adinkra fabrics have been produced by machine prints and modern batik methods which mainly use synthetic dyes. But artisans of Ntonso (Adinkra craft village) still use some natural dyes for their work. They also use traditional methods of making the cloth.

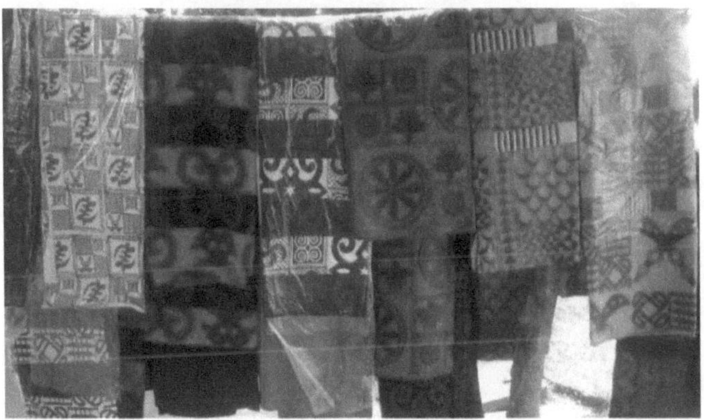

Adinkra fabrics

To begin the process of making the cloth traditionally, the artisan would first need to have his hand-woven cloth in place if he intends to hand-print symbols on cloth. If artisan prefers a different colour background aside from the white cloth, the cloth must be dyed first to whatever colour preferred before printing is done. In case he intends to do an embroidery of symbols or weaving of symbols in cloth as in Kente, he would have to dye threads first in the preferred dye.

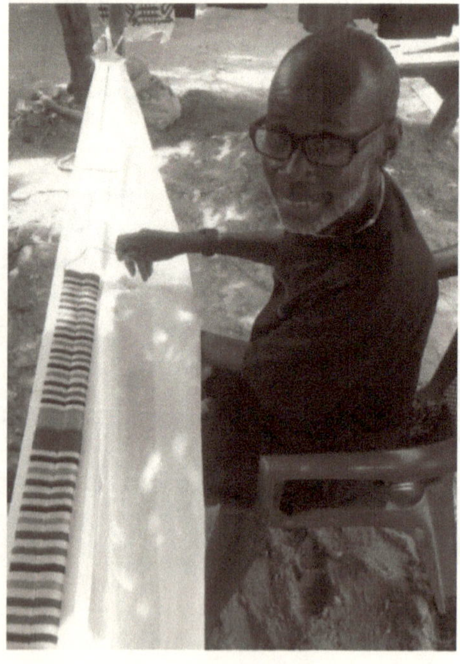

Embroidery

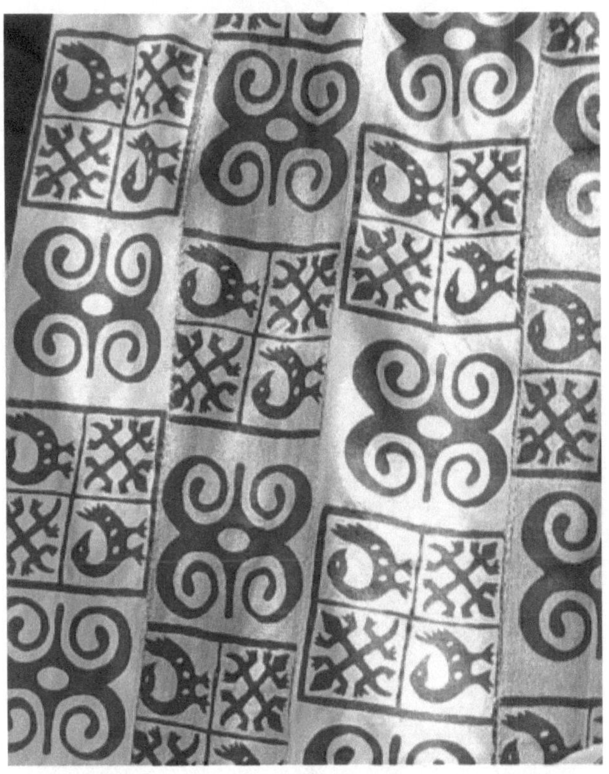

Printed Adinkra patterns

In the past, Adinkra symbols were carved on pieces of gourd. This is still being practised here. This gourd is originally a hard-shell, green inedible fruit of a vine. After harvesting this fruit, it is cut open and the inner part scooped out. It is then left under the sun to dry for days until it turns all brown and hard for the artisan to create his desired Adinkra symbols with it. These carved symbols shown below can be used for several years. Gourd has also been used in ancient West Africa and present-day for creating musical instruments such as xylophone. The carved Adinkra symbols are dipped in dyes and ink processed from trees (plants) and printed on cloth when making Adinkra fabric traditionally.

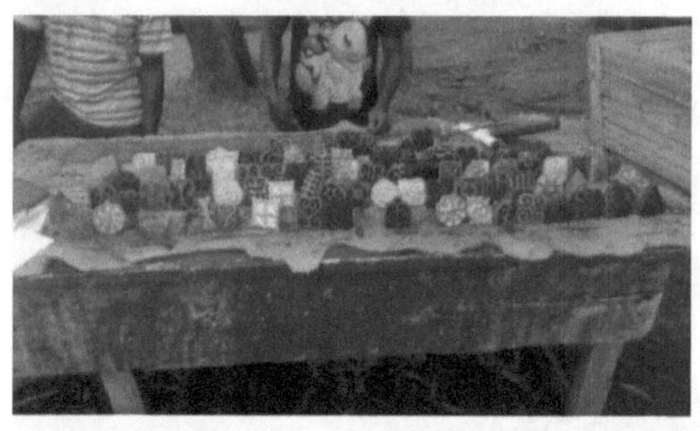

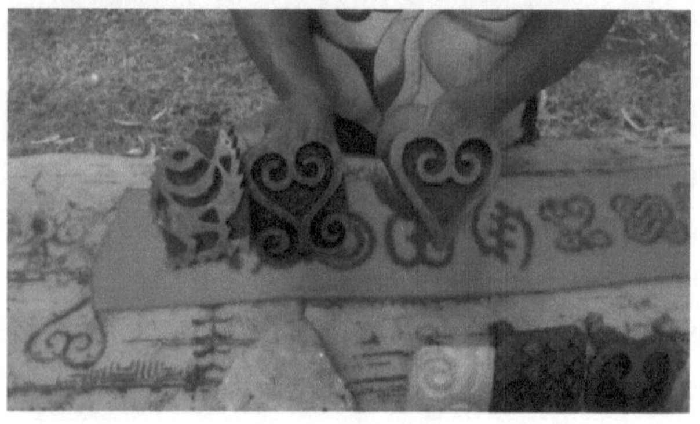

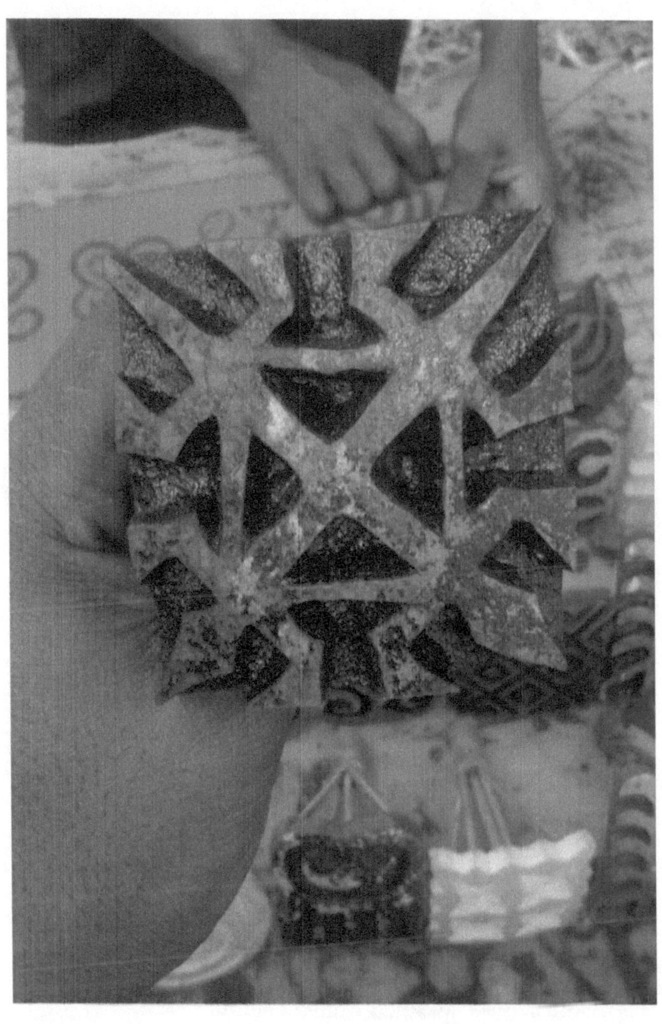

Adinkra symbol

Before the use of plants, mud was used specifically to dye Adinkra cloths here. One tree that served as a source of colour for Adinkra and still used by artisans in Ntonso is the Badie tree. The artisan extracts colour from the bark of this tree by first breaking it into pieces and then soaking it in water for 24 hours. After the 24 hours in the water, the solution turns brownish, the artisan tells me this means it is ready. The pieces are then removed, placed in a mortar and pounded with a pestle into fine grains. It is then transferred into a pot of water and cooked for 4 hours. After 4 hours, the solution turns reddish-brown and the artisan takes it off the fire. He sieves out the rough particles from the solution and cooks the smooth solution for an extra 4 hours until it evaporates and forms a thick solution. This final solution then serves as the ink to be used for hand printing or stamping symbols on the cloth. The Badie ink used for Adinkra serves as a source of black colour which is stamped on a plain white background or coloured background of cloth. As indicated earlier, this was done on hand-woven cloth in the past since it was the cloth available but now it is also done on ready-made cloth. The Badie ink is also called Adinkra aduru.

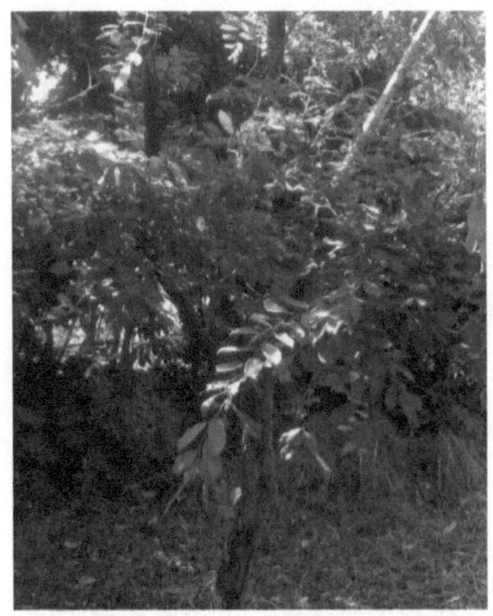

Badie tree

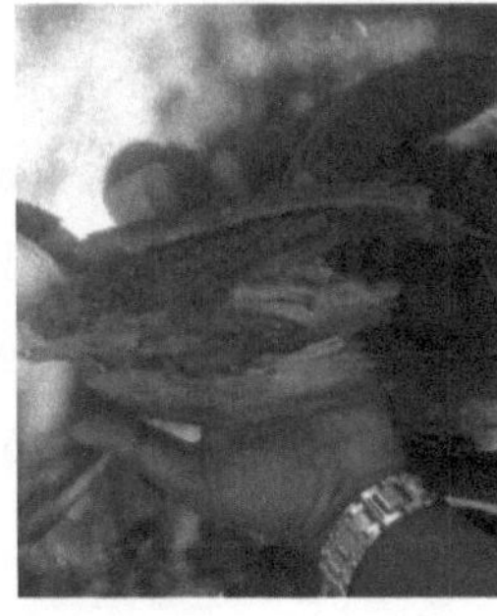

Bark of the tree

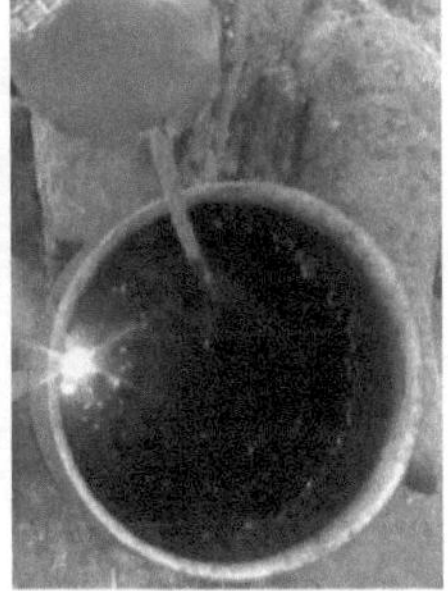

Badie ink

To have a cloth dyed reddish-brown colour (a ceremonial Ashanti mourning cloth), before stamping symbols with the ink, the roots and bark of a tree known as Kuntunkuni (*Bombax Brevicuspe*) are used for dyeing. They are boiled for hours and cloth dipped in solution for some time and dried. The cloth is repeatedly soaked in the dye bath and dried until artisan gets the desired shade of colour. I have been informed this is the same process used in the past for dyeing cloths into other colours as well. Roots of the Baobab tree (*Adansonia Digitata)* can be used for red. Other plants such as the roots and stem of a vine called Avumansaka by Ewes, can be used for a red shade. They grind the stem of the plant and mix it in water, the cloth is then left in the solution for a day. A plant known as Kanee was used in the past for yellow dyeing. All these plants also undergo the boiling process of extracting dye. Some of these dye plants including the indigo plant are also used by indigenous herbalists in these parts for medicinal purposes. In present-day, red, yellow and other colour backgrounds of Adinkra cloth are no longer done traditionally but with synthetic dyes. Only russet brown dyeing (kuntunkuni) and the black ink (adinkra aduru) are still traditionally done by some artisans.

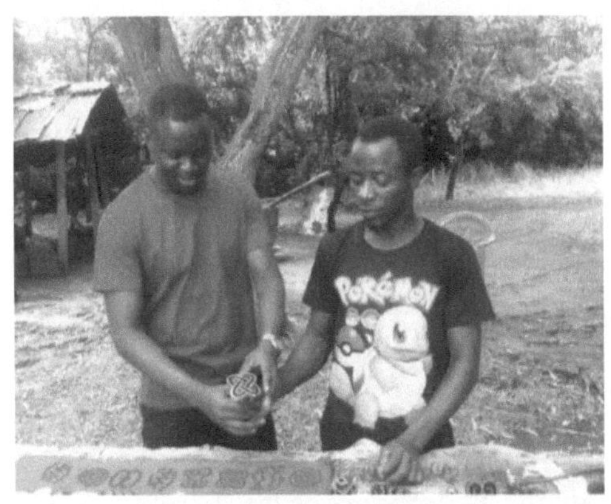

Stamping symbols on cloth

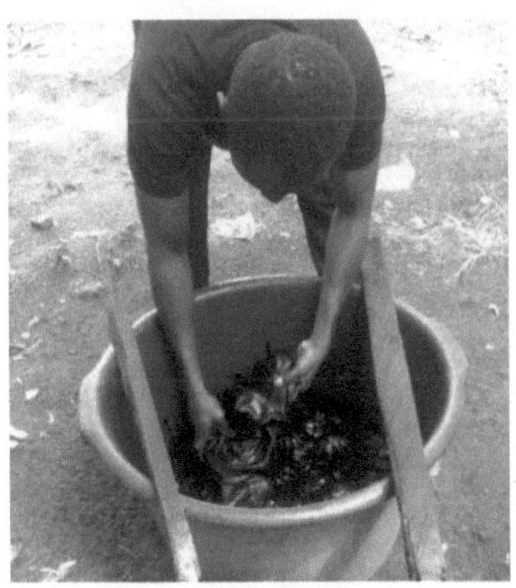

Natural Kuntunkuni dyeing

Akans are believed to have migrated from the Sahel region of Africa. As common with the medieval era in Africa, Akans migrated to parts of West Africa for settlement just as some other ethnic groups at the time. As at the 13th century, the Akan Kingdom of Bonoman was already established and is accepted as the origin of other Akan subgroups who migrated out in search of gold, a commodity that started to boom in Bonoman. At a period when the Mali Empire was experiencing a recession, Bonoman and other Akan states filled the void as major players in the gold trade of the region. Bonoman and other Akan states are the predecessors of the Ashanti (Asante) kingdom. This kingdom is the pillar of Adinkra and also the most popular of Akan kingdoms. It was founded in 1670 by King Osei Tutu I by unifying some Akan states. It was known for its gold trade, kente and rich culture. Gold dust was a medium of exchange in Ashanti and the kingdom wielded great influence in West Africa. The most important cultural element of the kingdom is the Golden Stool conjured from the sky by the chief priest Okomfo Anokye according to legend. It is the unifying force, the ultimate symbol of power and the royal throne of the Ashantis.

Ashantis designed their Kente mainly with geometric patterns as we have seen earlier, before they were introduced to Adinkra symbols after their conquest of the Jaman (Gyaman) kingdom. Ever since, kente has also been designed with Adinkra patterns. It is unclear the exact date Adinkra cloth came into existence in Akan culture before being introduced to Ashanti between 1800 and 1803. But it is believed to have been made even before the 1700s. One early example of Adinkra cloth can be found in the British Museum, collected in 1817 by Thomas Edward Bowditch. It was collected on his journey to Kumasi, capital of the Ashanti Kingdom now Ghana's Ashanti Region. The present-day ruling monarch is King Osei Tutu II. The residence of the sovereign is the Manhyia Palace in Kumasi. Bowditch recorded details of the journey which was even before the series of Anglo-Ashanti wars in his 1819 book, *Mission from Cape Coast Castle to Ashantee*

According to oral tradition, Adinkra symbols were revealed to a Jaman king called Kwadwo Adinkra Agyemang in a dream. Jaman was a former kingdom covering from the Brong Ahafo region to present-day neighbouring Ivory Coast. It was also made up of an Akan group. This king drew the symbols on a gourd as they had been revealed to him in the dream and later presented them to his chiefs and family members with their interpretations. These revelations came at a time that there was discord in the royal household, thereby threatening peace in the entire kingdom. He was successful in using the symbols along with their interpretations to suppress the ensuing hostilities. These symbols bear proverbs, folktales, philosophy and even myths. Right from their inception in the kingdom of Jaman, they were regarded sacrosanct.

Many years after the reign of Kwadwo Adinkra Agyemang, there came a later successor around the late 1700s named Nana Kofi Adinkra. By Ashanti history, he provoked the Ashanti kingdom to war by claiming he has in his possession the same golden stool as that of the Ashanti kingdom. This may seem trivial but to appreciate the severity of his utterance you would have to really understand the concept of the golden stool and also traditional stool in the broader sense of West African traditional society. Across most West African cultures, the traditional stool is of great importance and there are different stools for different purposes. This is one reason why one can see various stool motifs present in some traditional African textiles. They are seen as relics passed down from generation to generation and very much revered. Even some families (clans) in some West African societies who practise the African traditional religion own family stools. Traditional stools are used mainly in installing a monarch in these societies. This is a very old practise and still exists in the present day. For instance, it is said that one group (family) of Ewes forgot their stool in Notsie during the migration and had to send two members back in disguise to retrieve it. These individuals' family lines were said to have been inducted into ruling houses as a reward for returning the stool. The fact that they were willing to risk their lives for this stool says a lot about its significance to them. Another instant, is the European traveller who visited the kingdom of Dahomey at a time and described how their king's (King Guezo) stools were decorated with precious metals symbolizing his royal authority. It was not an ordinary craftsman who crafted traditional stools of this calibre but those with deep knowledge in the traditional religion. It could be cast in metal or carved out of wood. And they have also come to be considered as works of art in their own right. Even though traditional stool was that important to other African cultures, it can be argued that what the golden stool meant to the Ashanti people was something else. It is their premium stool and considered as their very existence as a nation. They believe it holds the spirits of their ancestors and even that of those yet to be born. It is handled by the king himself and it does not touch the ground. The stool is seen occasionally during some festivals where it is placed on a throne next to the king. It is taken back to a hidden location known only to the king, queen mother and trusted council members. It is said that the Ashanti king sits on a golden stool so some mistake it in literal terms. Even during his installation as a king, he is only lowered and raised over it in a gesture to show he occupies it but actually, he does not touch it. The stool is believed to have landed on the laps of the first king when it was conjured from the sky. This was proof to the subjects that he had been chosen by the gods to be king over the united Akan states. This is why another king's (Nana Kofi Adinkra) claim of possessing the golden stool could not be taken lightly. It was a challenge to the legitimacy of the Ashanti king at the time and was also a pronouncement that the Jaman kingdom is as powerful as the Ashanti kingdom. To possess the stool means to possess the kingdom of Ashanti, making this pronouncement a declaration of war at the time. This Jaman king would lose the war in the early 1800s and be marched to the Ashanti kingdom where he would also lose his life. The Jaman kingdom would then be annexed to the Ashanti kingdom and the two kingdoms unified under one ruler, King Osei Kwame Panyin (King of the Ashantis). Adinkra, as the name suggests, was named after the Jaman king (Nana Kofi Adinkra). He wore an "Adinkra" patterned garment while being taken to Ashanti. These symbols not common to Ashantis then would be interpreted as the defeated king's way of expressing sorrow on being taken away from home. Synonymous to a farewell (goodbye) posture. In Twi (Akan language) the word Adinkra stands for goodbye.

The Ashantis would then trace the symbols back to Jaman and adapt them. Due to the sorrow associated with the patterned garment of the Jaman king, it would first come to represent funeral cloth in Ashanti culture. But later come to represent more than that to them. These Adinkra symbols would then become an integral part of the Ashanti culture.

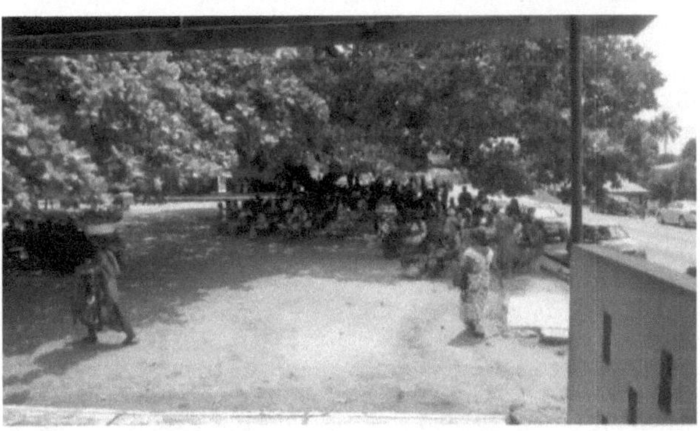

Adinkra worn at a funeral service in the Ashanti region

Adinkra cloth would come to serve as a significant means of communication in Ashanti and Akan culture as a whole. Adinkra symbols would give a particular voice to cloth and garment worn. It would first come to be associated with the royals and priests of the Ashanti kingdom, worn during festivities and on sacred ceremonies. It is reasonable to presume Adinkra cloth was first associated with royals because it was popularized in Ashanti by a king (Nana Kofi Adinkra). The symbols are also revered because they are believed to have been revealed to the ancient Jaman king (Kwadwo Adinkra Agyemang) from above. Even when Adinkra cloth became popular among all categories of people, symbols placed on a cloth to be worn were carefully selected by the wearer to convey a specific message when worn. Adinkra cloths are used mainly on occasions such as the naming ceremony of a newborn, Akan festivals, weddings and as usual funerals. During marriage ceremonies, not only is it worn but also in most cases forms part of the dowry from the groom to his bride. Red, black and brown colours of Adinkra cloth are associated with funerals but a mixture of the black and white background is also accepted for funerals especially when the deceased died at the old age due to natural causes. This makes it a form of celebration of life, like a 91-year-old's funeral I witnessed here. The colour red symbolizes death and black sadness in Ashanti culture. White – purity, green – growth and good health, yellow – precious and the colour gold represents royalty and wealth. White, yellow and other bright coloured Adinkra cloth are normally associated with festive occasions and categorized as Kwasiada Adinkra. Kwasiada Adinkra stands for merry cloth and is considered inappropriate for funerals. Till date, the Adinkra cloth is worn by the Ashanti king on festivals. The symbols on his cloth also serve as a means of communication to Asanteman (means Asante-state in Twi).The type of cloth worn could depict the mood of the kingdom. In past times, it could even serve as strategic communication for military advances, similar to the traditional dance and Akan talking drum which was a major channel of communication. By the beat of the drum, the sovereign could communicate anything he wanted to his people which will just be music in the ears of a stranger. One of the most popular of Adinkra symbols is the Gye Nyame symbol which represents the supremacy of God. It is so widely used and accepted that it can be seen even on church buildings. Over the years, other variations of the main symbols of Adinkra would come up, Ashantis would develop additional symbols incorporating their art and culture which would all come to be accepted as Adinkra symbols. I would like to mention that there are more Adinkra symbols than the ones covered below and that few of the symbols are no longer relevant in the present-day state of affairs in Ashanti culture.

Adinkra Symbols and Meanings

Adinkrahene (Adinkra King): Chief of all designs. Symbolizes leadership and forms the basis of Adinkra printing.

Nea onnim no sua a, ohu: He who does not know can know from learning. Symbolizes lifelong education.

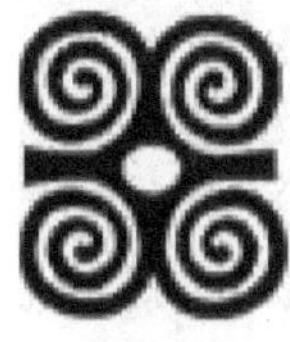

Dwannimen (Ram's horn): It is the heart and not the horn that leads a ram to bully.

Ese ne tekrema (The teeth and the tongue): We improve and advance together. Symbolises Friendship.

Nyame dua :Tree of God. Symbolizes God's protection.

Sankofa (To go back for something): Symbolizes going back for a forgotten tradition or policy.

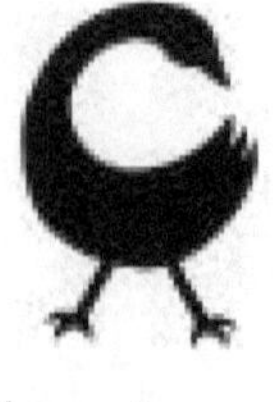 Sankofa. (Another version): Learning from the past.

Krado- mmra krado (Seal of law and order): Symbolizes the authority of the court.

Odo nnyew fie kwan: Love never loses its way. Symbolizes the power of love.

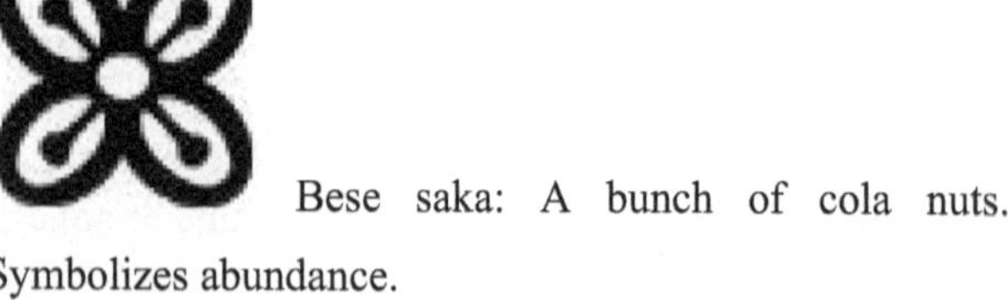 Bese saka: A bunch of cola nuts. Symbolizes abundance.

Mframadan (Wind house): House built to stand windy and treacherous conditions. Symbolizes fortitude.

Ohene tuo. (The king's gun): Defender of the king.

Akoma ntoaso: Symbol of agreement or charter.

Odenkyem da nsuo mu, nso onnhome nsuo, ohome mframa: The crocodile lives in water yet it breathes air, not water.

Owo foro adobe. (A snake climbing a palm tree): Performing the unusual or impossible.

Kete pa: Good bed. Symbolises good marriage.

Gye Nyame (Except God): Symbol of the omnipotence and immortality of God.

Nyame nwu na mawu: If God dies then I may die. Symbolises dependence on God.

Gyawu atiko: This is said to be the haircut of Gyawu, a past hero and chief of the town Bantama in Ashanti.

Pempamsie (That which will not crush): Unity is strength.

Nyansapo: Symbol of wisdom and intelligence.

Boa me na me mmoa wo: Help me and let me help you. Symbolizes the spirit of cooperation.

Kra pa Mmusuyide: Symbol of good fortune and sanctity.

Akoma (The Heart): Symbol of patience and endurance.

Aban (Fence): Symbol of protection or safety.

Ntesie- mate masie: I have heard and kept quiet. Symbol of knowledge.

Nsaa (a kind of blanket): Symbol of excellence.

Wawa Aba: Symbol of strength. Seed of the Wawa tree. Wawa is a hardwood used for carving.

Ananse ntontan: Spider's web. Symbolizes creativity.

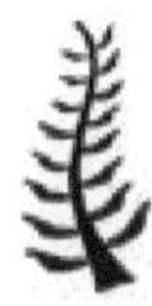 Nyame nti: By God's grace.

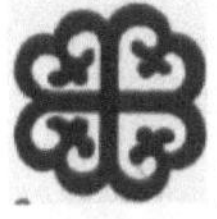 Nyamedua: An altar to the sky god.

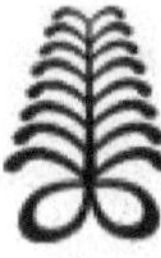 Aya, (the fern): A symbol of defiance.

Biribi wo soro: God, there is something in the heavens let it reach me. Symbol of hope.

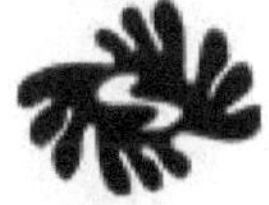 Bi nka bi: Bite not one another.

Nkyinkyim: Changing oneself. Playing many roles. Symbolizes dynamism and adaptability.

Nhwimu (Crossing): The crossed divisions made on some Adinkra cloth before stamping. Symbol of skillfulness and precision.

Mpuannum (Five tufts of hair): Symbolises a priestly office.

Osrane ne Nsoroma (Moon and star): Symbol of faithfulness.

Fihankra (The complete house): Symbol of safety or security in a home.

Krammo bonne amma yeanhunu kramo pa: Cannot tell the good from the bad.

Duafe: The wooden comb symbolises feminine virtue. (Everlasting love).

Akoko nan tia ba, na nkum ba: The hen treads upon its chicken but does not kill them.

Hwemudua (Quality Control): Symbol of Quality.

Afena :A state ceremonial sword. A retiring great warrior always has a royal sword of rest.

mpatapo: Knot of reconciliation. Symbolizes peace.

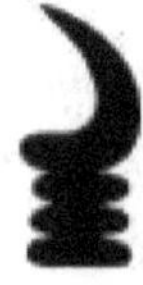

Asase ye duru: Symbolizes divinity of mother Earth.

Funtumfunafu denkyemfunafu: Siamese crocodile. Sharing one stomach yet they fight over food Symbolises the need for unity.

Pa gya (To strike fire or make fire): This is said to represent war.

Kuntinkantan (Do not boast): There is the need for humility and service.

Ako- ben (War horn): Symbol of a call to arms.

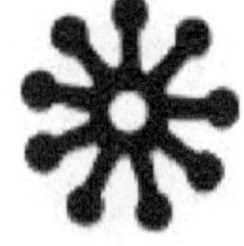 Epa (Handcuffs): You are the slave of him whose handcuffs you wear.

 Owuo atwedie baako mmfo: All men shall climb the ladder of death.

Fofoo: Symbol of Jealousy.

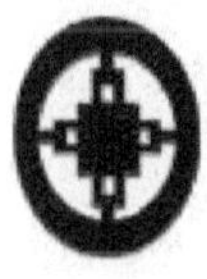 Nkonsonkonson (Link of Chain): Symbol of human relations.

Nsoroma (star): Child of the heavens.

Dame- dame: A draft game.

Nkwuma kesee: Symbol of superiority.

Kontire (Tikoro nko agyina): One head does not make a council. Symbolizes a ruler must lead with the guidance of a council.

Nea ope. : Do unto others what you wish be done to you. Symbolizes justice.

Me ware wo: I would marry you. Symbolizes commitment.

I believe as the Jaman king Nana Kofi Adinkra made that final journey to Ashanti, he never suspected he would become the greatest export of his kingdom. He must have thought of the disappointment that had come of his reign and ponder what might become of his kingdom and culture.

He would have never known he was going along with a tradition on his back that would be embraced and passed on generations after generations to this day. As one Adinkra symbol above implies, Death comes to all living. To some cultures, what matters is what piece of us lives on long after we are gone. It may take any form, be it a legacy, through a tradition, through a child or even through a piece of cloth. This king might not have had a golden stool that could rival the power of the Ashantis, but a tradition that would be worthy of their respect. Today Adinkra symbols are widely used and have become part of our daily lives. We see them not only in fabrics but in logos, architecture, jewellery and furniture among others here in West Africa and other parts of the world.

5

MUD CLOTH/ BOGOLAN

Mud cloth making involves the use of special clay preserved for a year with some water. A piece of this old mud (clay) is scooped and mixed in a bowl of water to make a uniform solution which is then used for dyeing purposes. For the yellow colour in mud cloth, leaves of the trees known as N'galaman (*Anogeissus leiocarpa)* and N'tjankara (combretum glutinosum) are used. These are tropical West African trees. Leaves of these trees are pounded just like the bark of the Badie tree in a mortar and later boiled for some minutes when making the dye. The cotton cloth to be used for the mud cloth is then dipped in the solution for some time. This cloth later turns from its original cream or white to yellow.

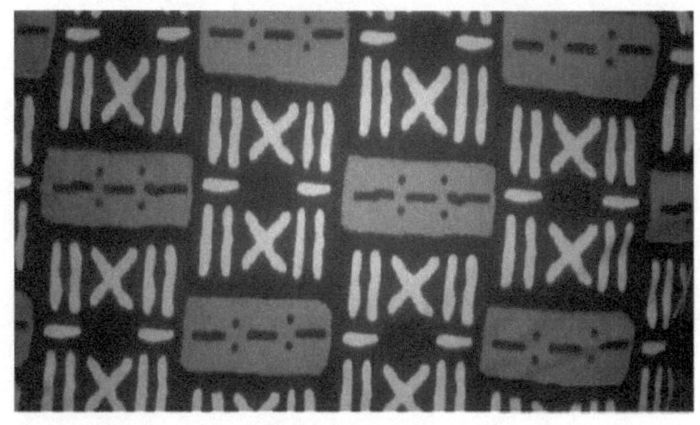

Mud cloth

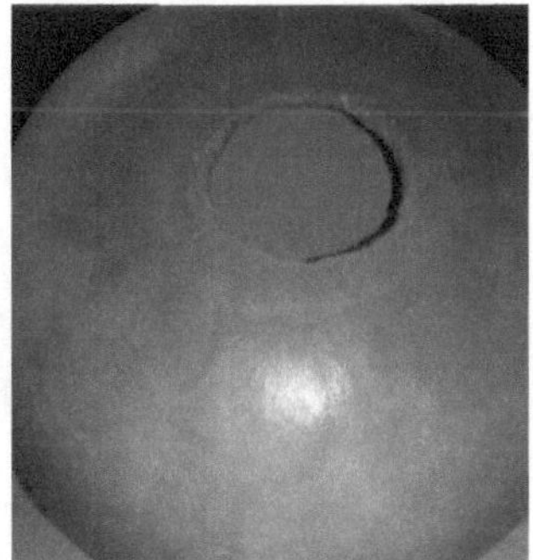

storage of mud

The cloth is then left under the sun for a long period so it can be brighter. It is as if the yellow colour feeds on the sunshine for its brightness. I observed the same practise with contemporary batik craftswomen after dyeing the yellow colour in synthetic dyes. After the cloth is dried, the artisan applies the designs and the old mud solution diluted into uniform paste is applied to portions of the design where it is needed. After the tedious process of designing the cloth, it is dried again and when the mud dries fully, the cloth is rinsed in a bowl of water for drying. When dried the cloth is dipped one more time in the traditional yellow dye solution. There are other methods also used in making mud cloth aside this one.

Motifs of mud cloth can be found in abstract and figurative forms. Mud cloth has its roots in the ancient Mali Empire. I was told that the cloth is as old as the former empire itself. It is regarded as a tradition inherited from the forbears. In the Bamana culture of Mali, hunters wore the cloth for protection from bad spirits in the forest. It is believed that some unknown forces live in forests. This is one assertion some other cultures share. There is a known adage in one West African language that; "A hunter does not talk about everything he sees in the forest". Some types of mud cloth were also used as special cloth by young women during certain periods in their life such as puberty. It also has various ceremonial uses in Malian culture. The old Mali was a West African empire that existed from the 13th century to the 17th century and is also a succeeding empire to the former Ghana Empire. Present-day Ghana was named after the ancient Ghana empire by its founding fathers because of the belief that some of the ethnic groups had migrated from there. This was based on a theory the Arab philosopher and historian Ibn Khaldun proposed in his book. He believed most of the people there had relocated to the other parts of Africa for settlement after the fall of the empire. The Mali Empire was founded by Sundiata Keita and was famous for its wealth and power. The empire controlled gold trade in the entire region of Africa and it was also one of the largest gold producers in the region at a point in time. Mansa Musa was a later king of Mali and because of his kindness, the price of gold drastically reduced in parts of the Middle East when he made his holy trip to Mecca. He was a very generous man and gifted many people with gold during this pilgrimage. He travelled with many escorts who loaded ounces of gold on their camels, so he could give alms to the poor. This led to the devaluation at the time.

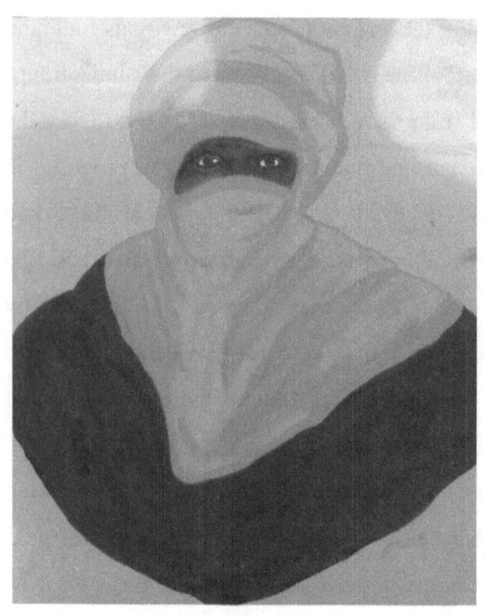

A depiction of Mansa Musa

He made this trip after he succeeded King Abu Bakr II, an explorer who did not return from a sailing expedition. Mansa Musa was a devout Muslim and a lover of knowledge. News of his golden pilgrimage to Mecca spread so much that it even went across the Mediterranean. This is believed to have led to him being immortalized overseas in the ancient Catalan Atlas (Spanish map), where he is depicted holding a golden orb on a golden throne.

It is not for no reason that some of the old African relics such as the centuries-old indigo threads were found in

Mali. Their history with the indigo cloth is already known. The Arab traveller Ibn Battuta even made mention of the distinct blue cloth on his voyage to the empire in his days in the 14th century. Another Portuguese explorer Duarte Pacheco Pereira wrote in 1506 about the kingdom's wealth of gold and also does not fail to mention the blue cloth. African textiles have always had a strong presence in African societies. The fact that these explorers would take notice of these fabrics aside all other things they might have forgotten to mention goes to prove this point. These textiles are a form of identity, this reminds me of the man in Northern Ghana who told me indigo dyeing has a long-standing tradition in his family and part of his people's identity. He is right to have said so because he is of Gonja ancestry and Gonja people are descended from people who migrated from the Mali Empire and settled in parts of Northern Ghana. One issue I was confronted with was brought forward by a fellow who believed that the Hausas might have introduced the Gonjas to the practise of indigo dyeing itself and not only the pit method as they claim. We were both later convinced that it could not have been possible since the Gonja people had come from a strong indigo dyeing tradition. Only the method might have been different. Mali is a very important kingdom in West African history and has had a significant influence on many

West African groups. Let us take for instance, northern Ghana, you would notice that the Gonjas are not the only tribe there with Malian ancestors and aside from this part of Ghana, other West African countries too were settled by groups of people from Mali. There are other migrations that might have occurred earlier than these ones. Some later historians also strongly believe the mass migrations of people that occurred in the Ghana Empire era for instance were directed to the forest regions of West Africa. This is also because most of the settlements in the forest regions are relatively new when comparing them to others. These migrations highlights the possibility of shared culture at a point in history between some groups. This would explain similarities of culture between groups that are not known to have any relationship. The Mali Empire was one of the first empires in Africa and the world to be converted to Islam, therefore having a firm base in Islamic tradition and knowledge. Timbuktu was the hub of knowledge in the Mali Empire and an important zone of scholarship in the Muslim world. It hosted one of the early universities in the world known as the Sankore University, and one could study several disciplines there. Till date, several old manuscripts turn up by the day in present-day Mali. Aside from the university, there were other Maliki schools which offered pre-tertiary education. The Mali Empire had a strong presence in the region and even controlled points of entry to sub-Saharan Africa. They had an organized military, strong alliances and diplomatic missions across strategic areas of the region. Aside from Islamic culture, there was also strong traditional African culture prevailing, which was promoted by some kings who were traditional adherents. An example is Sonni Ali Ber whose kingdom later absorbed the Mali Empire. The Portuguese explorer also observed the prevalence of red cloth which I suspect was made out of dyes extracted from the Baobab as was done in the past by other West African traditions as mentioned earlier. It is a widely known source of red dye. This Baobab tree in itself is important in Malian tradition. It has a foundation deep-rooted in Malian oral tradition. In the epic of Sundiata (Tales of Mali Empire), griots record that Sundiata, the founder of Mali who was born unable to walk began to walk when he used part of the Baobab.

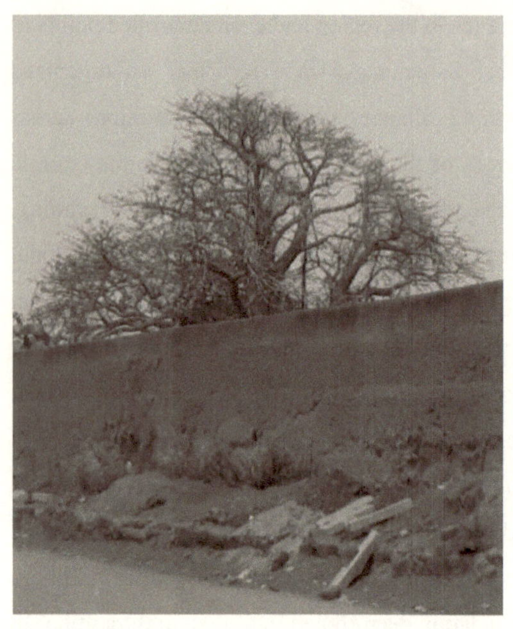

Baobab tree

There are many West African folklores specifically about the tree. This tree is native to West Africa and is highly respected in West African societies. It is a gigantic tree with a long life span. It can grow to about 3000 years. Trees of this category were also considered deities. Even in the past kingdom of Dahomey, there was a culture of giving special status to some trees as well. These trees were very much revered and cutting them down was a taboo.

6

KORHOGO CLOTH

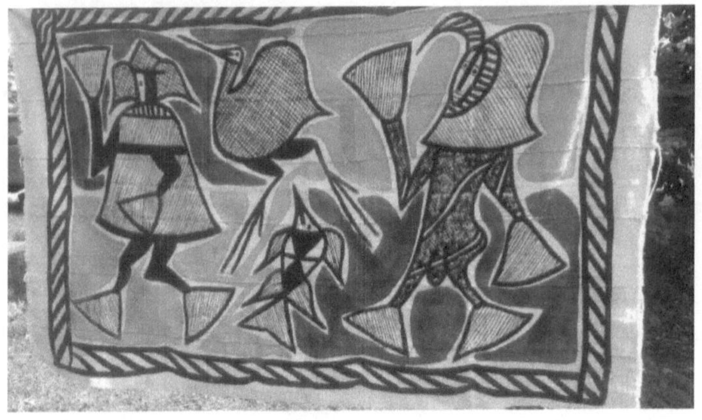

The Korhogo cloth of Ivory Coast is very much similar to
the mud cloth of Mali, which is why people often mistake
the two. The Korhogo cloth is done by the Senufo people.
When making the cloth, they prefer to draw their tribal
symbols (designs) with stencils directly on hand-woven
cloth. They also hand paint natural dyes directly on the
cloth. The designs are made on strips of traditional woven
cloth sewn together. It is dyed with the same mud dyeing
method as the Mud cloth discussed earlier. Motifs used for
the cloth come in form of animals, masquerades, masks,

102

humans and other inspirations from nature such as celestial bodies. There is said to be about 100 motifs. A motif of Fish represents life or water, guinea fowl represents beauty, chicken represents motherhood, lion- royal power and chameleon represents death. The masquerades displayed on this cloth come in different forms which are intriguing to watch. Masquerades are closely associated with numerous West African cultures. I have seen various masquerade performances during my travels, especially on some traditional festival grounds. These masquerades often represent an object of worship. However, this is the first West African textile tradition that I have seen that uses motifs of masquerades.

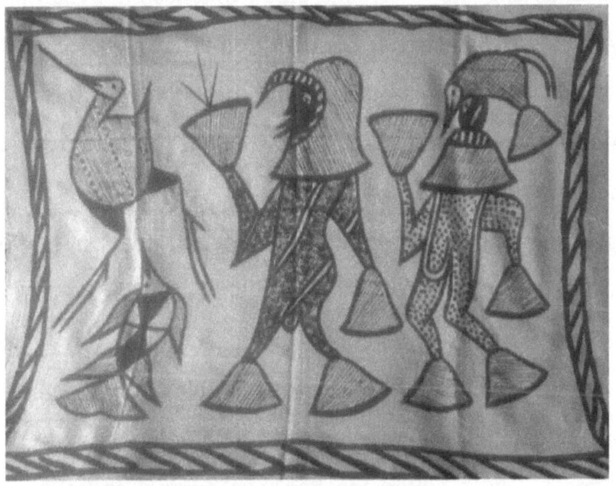

Korhogo cloth

These symbols stem from the myths and belief system of the people. They are old artistic expressions deep-rooted in their traditional customs. They were used in decorating buildings in the past just as Adinkra symbols were used in Ashanti for decorating buildings as observed by Thomas Edward Bowditch during his visit. Just as practised in other West African cultures, women do the plucking of cotton and spinning to yarns and the men do the weaving. The one difference here is that the women also prepared the dyes for the painting on cloth as the case in Mali when making Mud cloth. One can presume these artists painted on walls of buildings and over time their art was infused with their textiles and other mediums. Observing the different designs and motifs of this cloth, one sees a signature of African art which can be identified at first glance. In the olden days, natives believed the inclusion of some of the motifs in the cloth made it a powerful protection for the owner from evil forces. It could be worn and also hanged at homes. The Senufo are a people found in northern Ivory Coast and a few also live in neighbouring West African countries. They are a conservative society that developed their own education system. Their schools were gender-based with both sexes having separate school systems. The female school called the Sandogo society and the male referred to as the Poro society. These schools equipped young ones with the knowledge and skills needed in life. They also served as a means of transferring culture to the next generation. They had different craft schools and took these schools seriously, studying the traditional crafts and art years before finally graduating. They were only allowed to use some motifs of Korhogo in their work after graduation. This shows how important the motifs are to them.

Some of the most important motifs are masks. These masks are created by the best artists of this society who also fall in a category of highly respected individuals. They are regarded as gifted people. To these people, art is spiritual, in other words, it can transcend the physical realm. The motifs of the korhogo cloth are not limited to only fabrics but are used in other mediums such as sculpture and pottery. I have noticed some of their mask motifs bear striking resemblance to other West African masks and it seems as if these artists were inspired from the same source. It is said that some of these motifs inspired some works of Pablo Picasso, specifically his line of African Arts. The Korhogo cloth also was an important attire for hunters in the past just as the mud cloth in Malian culture. It also served as a traditional costume for graduating students from the schools of the society. The boys were considered men upon graduating from the school. The main object of worship of the Senufo people is feminine, unlike most African traditional cultures which are masculine. But one similarity is that, their main deity is also worshipped through lesser gods. These people also have a matrilineal inheritance system that is similar to that of the Ashantis, even though they live in a patriarchal society. They have a strong belief in life after death. They believe they still have connections with their ancestors.

BENIN APPLIQUE CLOTH

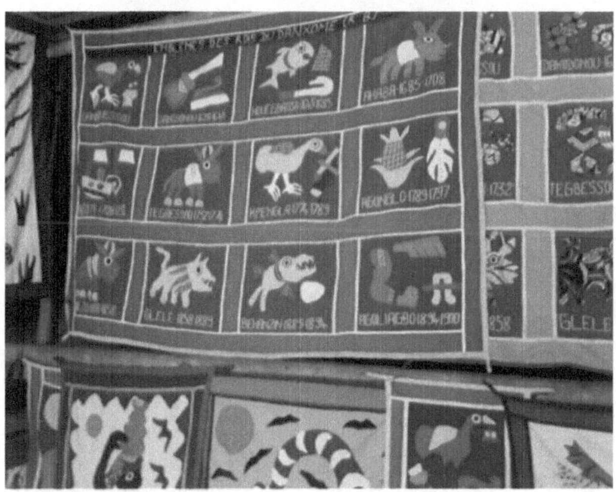

I am in Benin now admiring their beautiful Applique textile, this textile is done by stitching fabrics on other fabrics. Patterns are stitched skillfully that it is difficult to know at first sight. Threads are also used skillfully in the process of designing patterns on the cloth. The background cloth on which the stitching or embroidery is done can be hand woven, pieces of the hand woven cloth are then sewn together. The experts who make this cloth are men and referred to as Tisserand. The cloth was a form of a flag for the ruling monarchs of the kingdom, containing a king's attributes and achievements even before ascending the royal throne. The cloth is also worn, used as wall hangings, caps and to decorate umbrellas and tents as well. The Englishman Frederick E. Forbes witnessed a forty-foot tall tent decorated with Applique textiles during his 1850 visit to the Dahomey kingdom. A ceremonial applique textiles umbrella was made mainly for the king. A Dahomey king's umbrella was also crafted to serve as a fan that is propelled with manpower.

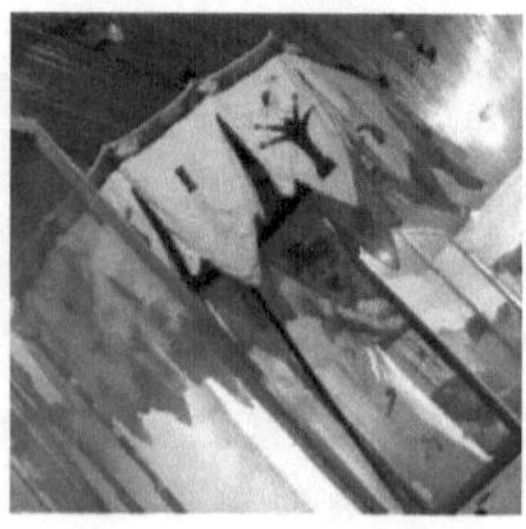

Ancient Dahomey applique Umbrella

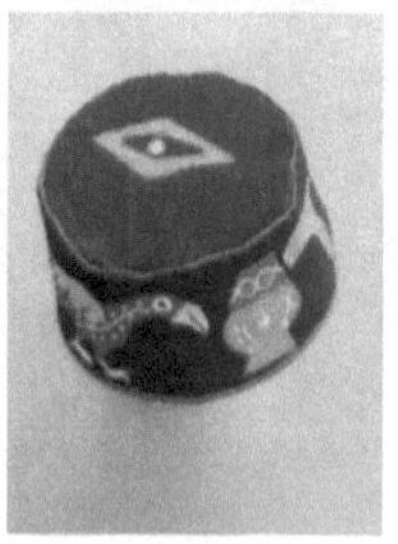

an applique Cap

The king sits under the umbrella when he is outdoors in the open and it is supposed to be propelled clockwise always. The clockwise propelling of the umbrella-fan is said to represent good fortunes, progress for the king and when propelled anti-clockwise stands for the opposite; bad fortune for the king. Types of the applique cloth were used on sacred ceremonies such as traditional initiation rites. The people of Abomey in Benin still regard it as a sacred cloth. It is a significant record of symbolic events in the history of Dahomey. Dahomey was a West African kingdom that existed from the early 17th century to the 19th century made up of a subgroup of the Gbe language speakers; Fon and Aja people. The Gbe language speakers had migrated from present-day Nigeria, neighbouring the Oyo Empire of the Yoruba people before spreading out to various locations. This group and the Yoruba group have some shared history. The Yorubas are believed to be of Nile Valley origins. The Gbe language family are said to have paid homage to the Yoruba's Oyo Empire for some period during their stay in that geographical area. Later exodus would take them to present-day Benin, Togo and Ghana, different groups settling in these locations. The group that settled in Benin, started the Dahomey kingdom.

This kingdom would become a powerful West African state conquering other existing settlements on the Atlantic coast. Their prisoners of war were sold to European slave traders. They had a well-organized military force which also had a special wing known as Mino, made up of females. The word ''Mino'' means our mothers in the Fon language. They would come to be known by European travellers as Dahomey Amazons. This was a group of strong, skilful women trained for war. They were said to be equally as good as their male counterparts in the art of battle. To qualify as a member of Mino, the female candidate must have a very good height. They are also selected from the ages of 12 to 14 and trained for 10 years before graduating as a Mino. The last but not the least criteria to be met in the selection process is beauty. They say this attribute served as an advantage to the women soldiers since some men were confounded by it on the field of battle. In this culture, it is said that beauty is also considered a weapon. Women were accorded great respect in this society and it was considered prestigious to serve in the king's army. Dahomey had a good economy which was supported by extensive trade, agriculture and all sorts of craftsmanship. Businesses were taxed to fund social projects such as the construction of roads. The kingdom could boast of enormous art which is still evident in their old palace buildings, sculpture and textiles. The old royal palace complex can be located at Abomey with a few surviving buildings and walls serving as tourist sites. It has been designated as a UNESCO world heritage site and has been reserved as a museum (Historic Museum of Abomey). The palace infrastructure was usually big with several quarters for the king's household and other quarters for council meetings among others. The palace complex covered several hectares of land. The building's interior and pillars were decorated with bass-reliefs. Every newly installed King constructed his palace next to his predecessor's within the palace complex. This new palace symbolized a new reign and promise of further expansion of the kingdom. A king's palace was designed with his symbol (banner) in bass-relief sculptures. All kings had their totems and are represented by these totems even till this day. The Applique textile is decorated with totems of the past kings.

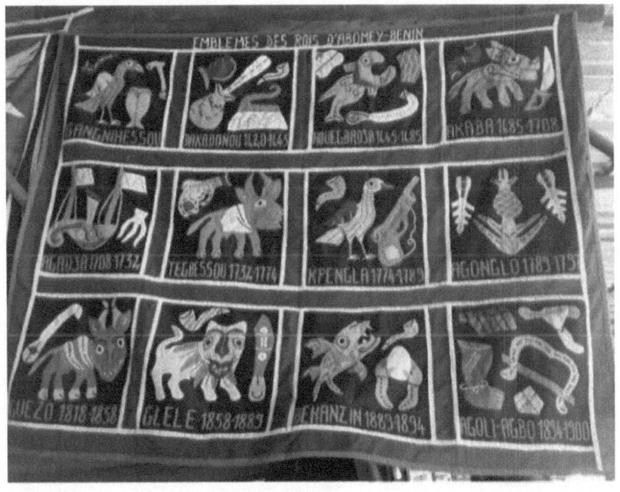

These totems have meanings. The first one which is represented by a bird. It is a bird known locally as Saswe, known for its greed. It depicts the first monarch, King Gangni Xesu (1620). This is largely because the man is believed to be a conqueror. He is credited as the founder of the kingdom of Dahomey. And this he was able to achieve by wanting more. He is said to have moved from another area before settling in the said area, but he would later start a dynasty which would cover the entire geographical location. Some griots also say he is known for leaving nothing to his opponents.

King Dako Donu (1620-1645) is represented by a jar of indigo. This is because he is known to have conquered an enemy who was preparing an indigo-dye in a jar. This enemy was said to have been a traditional leader who was known to be a strong man. This totem symbolized his victory and aura of domination. Dahomey also had a vibrant textiles industry, which comprised of cotton spinners, weavers and dyers. The indigo jar totem caught my attention in particular because it said a lot about the strong presence of indigo dyeing here too in the past. It can be said that Dahomey's rich textiles history continues till this day, evident with the presence of skilful weavers and beautiful traditional textiles. I noticed most applique textiles having different shades of indigo colours as a background colour.

The third, king Hwegbeadja (1645-1685) is represented by a fish trapped in a net. This refers to a dangerous trap he managed to overcome as a prince. This totem represents him as a personality that overcomes danger. This trap relates to him being disinherited by his father because he impregnated a woman who was betrothed to him. He was only reinstated as a king because he defeated an archenemy of his father. It was rare to be reinstated after being disinherited in this culture.

King Akaba (1685-1708) is symbolized by a chameleon. He is said to be the first son of his father, king Hwegbeadja. The history says he succeeded his father's throne at an old age. This led to people referring to his slowness as that of a chameleon. King Akaba is believed to have also contributed effectively in the expansion of the kingdom leading to some major changes in the regional structure that he inherited.

King Agadja (1708-1732) is represented by a boat because it was in his reign that European sailors arrived on the shores of Dahomey to trade. In his reign, the kingdom would become an important centre for trade along the coast. This is because of his attack on the other nearby settlements along the coast which had already established trading posts with the European traders. He would annex these settlements and make his kingdom the seat of government, in turn, becoming a very important part of the region.

King Tegbesu (1732-1774) is represented by a dressed-up buffalo because there was an attempt in his palace to poison his clothes. However, this plan did not succeed. This was one of the powerful kings that is why he is represented by a Buffalo. The animal represents strength and power here. He is known to have fought many successful battles that led to the expansion of the kingdom. It is believed he was not the first son of his father which would have normally disqualify him from becoming a successor but was appointed to be king because of his character of strength which is deserving of a king. Some West African cultures consider some specific traits in selecting a prince who would succeed the throne. There are also some actions that can disqualify a crowned prince. It is not always automatic for the firstborn to lead since there is a prevailing belief too that, royal leadership is a responsibility and not just a right.

It is why kingship can pass on to a younger brother. Even in the modern practise, this pattern recurs occasionally.

King Kpengla (1774-1789) is represented by a bird known as a war bird in Dahomey culture because of a battle that took place in the kingdom. This was largely a battle of succession. It was said that he invaded the palace with his army after the death of the king to lay claim on the throne. This led to a short-lived battle which ended up with him being victorious. It is believed at the time there was no clear favourite to succeed king Tegbesu. His reign began with a cry of war. Due to the circumstance surrounding his rise to power (enthronement), he is represented by the totem of the war bird.

King Agonglo (1789-1797) is represented by a pineapple because of his prudent and conservative nature. He is quoted to have said; anything small is not an easy target. This was a king who was not interested in extensive military campaigns but tried at some points in his reign and it did not go his way. He was said to be very careful in his dealings with others since he did not want unwarranted enemies. During his time as king, the kingdom did not experience any major expansion, this might also throw more light on the idea behind the totem. His reign was also marked with economic uncertainties which might have also played a role in his disposition.

King Guezo (1818-1858) is represented by a buffalo too because the animal is known to be powerful. It was his nature and opponents avoided encountering him because they were afraid of him. This was his way of keeping opponents from his kingdom. This king was as a clear contradiction to King Agonglo who was cool-headed. You would notice a gap in the reign between king Agonglo and king Guezo which is from 1797 to 1818. This was the reign of king Adandozan. He was toppled by king Guezo in a coup d'etat and king Guezo went on to erase him from the history of kings, this is a reason why his totem is not known. Because of this, King Adandozan is mostly overlooked when listing the kings of Dahomey. There are conflicting reports about why he was overthrown , for instance during my visit to the museum of Abomey in Dahomey, I was informed that he attempted to end the kingdom's slave trade which was already established at the time (also in his reign). In northern Ghana too, I was informed of a traditional leader called Kankrafu, who was so disgusted by the slave trade that he ended up sacrificing his life in an attempt to end the practise in his community. They say his action led to the deaths of the known slave traders (masters) of that region and also some of his trusted companions who stood beside him. His action went a long way in ending the practise there. There is reason to believe there was some level of tension in the later part of King Adandozan's reign which gave room for dissent within and outside the kingdom. This gave room for the coup and King Guezo had external support channeled through an important Brazilian merchant at the time called Francisco De Souza. He was also supported by other notable local personalities who had their own interest . These factions knew if anyone could overthrow the king it would be Guezo. He was the right man for the job and also related to the king. This throws more light on the nature of king Guezo. This king also liked to show off his power for all to see. A British sailor who visited the kingdom in this era also wrote about how the king showed off his wealth and power. During his reign, there were also threats from external forces and within the kingdom too. This is probably why he kept that posture throughout his time. Before he became king, the kingdom paid homage to the Oyo Empire, but after him, that was no more in effect. He ended that relationship in his time as a king, solidifying Dahomey's status as an independent kingdom. King Guezo was also said to be endowed with physical strength, he is believed to have killed a Buffalo without any help. This can be seen displayed in some Benin Applique arts.

King Glele (1858-1889) is represented by a lion because he was fierce and fearless. He was known to be a wild man bearing similarities with his predecessor king Guezo, who was also his father. This seems to have worked for him as well. A chip of the old block.

King Behanzin/Gbehanzin (1889-1894) represented by a shark and egg. It was in his reign that the kingdom suffered their defeat to France and later became a colony. This is why he is mostly referred to as the last king of Dahomey even though he was succeeded by King Agoli Agbo (1894-1900). This king is represented by a leg hitting a rock because he was enthroned by the French after king Behanzin was defeated. Starting from his reign, Abomey which was then the power hub of the kingdom struggled with its autonomy. He did not enjoy the power and authority of a sovereign ruler as enjoyed by his predecessors, he was rather regarded as a ceremonial leader. They also say he became king because none of the close relative of the ousted king Behanzin was willing to ascend the vacant throne.

King Behanzin is highly regarded in present-day Benin. This is also one of the reasons why he is popularly called the last king of Dahomey. He was a king known for his intolerance and hostility towards those who were his opponents. He was in turn qualified as a prideful and vindictive king by these opponents. However, he was also considered to be a wise king. King Behanzin was popular for his long smoking-pipe and is quoted to have said he was born smoking. The egg in his totem represents; "the universe holds the egg the earth deserves" and the shark; "the angry shark will terrorize its enemy". A warning to all who would try to oppose him. Though he commanded a formidable army of men, he was mostly guarded by the army of women referred to as Mino. His reign is marked for the many wars fought against the French army and their allied forces. The allied forces were made up of the other surrounding settlements who were not in good terms with the kingdom and had formed an alliance with France. This alliance was possible because during those periods, some West African kingdoms were embarking on expansion policies which resulted in the annexation of weaker states. The kingdom of Dahomey was no exception to the practise. This is even depicted in Dahomey arts, where Dahomey is represented as a huge bird swallowing a small bird (small states). This piece can be seen in the museum of Abomey.

The French and their allies fought some wars with Dahomey which lasted as long as two years. Some record of events blame King Behanzin for starting the hostilities by attacking neighbouring French colonies and arresting French officials. His response would be that "I am the king of blacks and whites have nothing to do with what I do. Settlements which you speak of are mine, they belong to me and I want them to be independent. I would like to know which independent French settlement was broken by me, King of Dahomey". King Behanzin finally lost the war and was exiled with his nuclear family to France and later Algeria where he would die. He is remembered in Benin for his fight against French colonialism. It must be mentioned that the Dahomey people believed in reincarnation of their kings, that is why when a king dies it was not referred to as death but rather as a night fall. There was a room where the next king had to commission a sacred monument made in honor of the deceased king, bearing his totem and lying next to his (deceased king) traditional stool. It is said that many of the Dahomey female warriors (Mino) fought fiercely and lost their lives in the last battle. The memory of King Behanzin inspired later insurrections in the colonial era that would finally lead to an independent present-day Benin (formerly the Dahomey kingdom). Though it is said that some of the female warriors found it difficult adjusting with their new life in a Dahomey-French colony, some were said to have gotten engaged in different types of trade. Some were known to have entered the craft of spinning cotton to yarns for making Applique textiles and the other hand woven Beninese textile. Making threads was a popular craft associated with women here at the time just as in other parts of West Africa. They also say a few of these women disguised themselves as wives of the brother of the exiled king Behanzin, serving as his protection. In a real sense, they were serving as the guardians of Dahomean tradition.

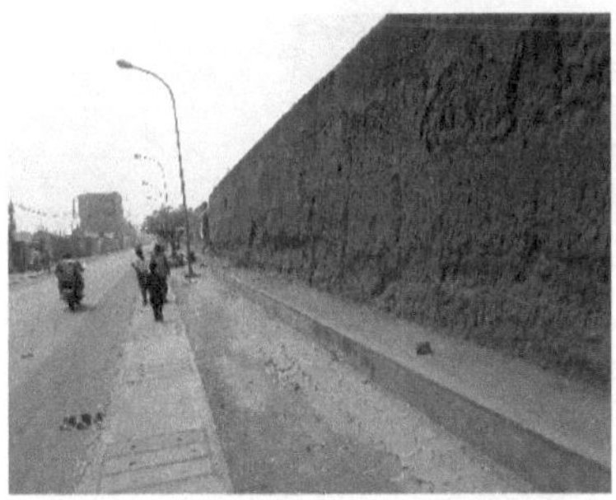

An ancient West African earth wall

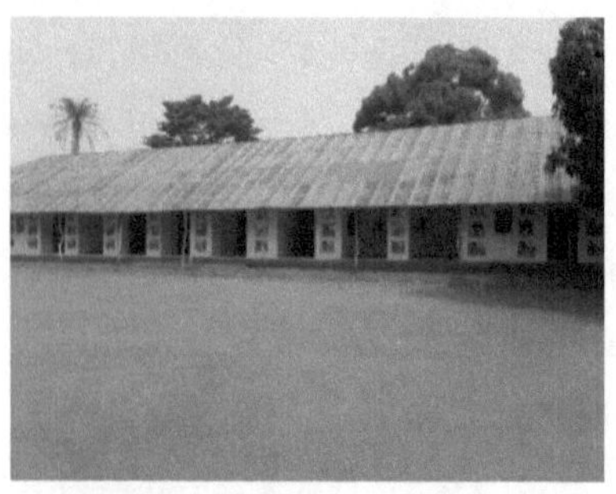

One old palace building on the complex, Abomey

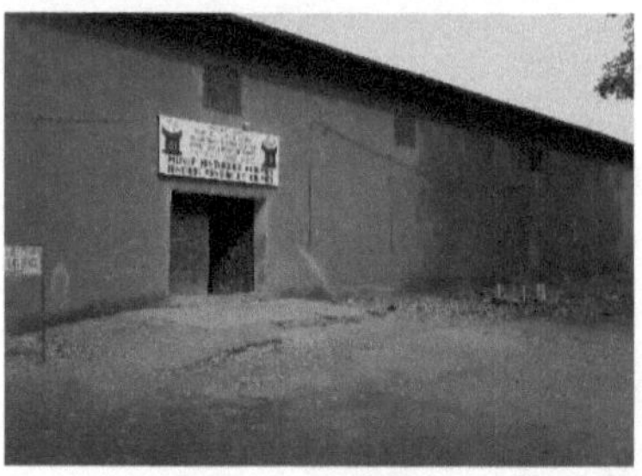

Entrance to one of the palace compounds

Benin is an interesting place to visit, the country has a rich tradition. It is mostly referred to as the origin of voodoo. That is why when I informed my friends I would be visiting the place, they made all sorts of jokes. Some asked whether I was going for charms. Others discouraged me saying it's a place full black magic and I could encounter spirits there. Of course, they had never been there themselves and had made up beautiful fantasies about the place from the little rumours they heard. I was later disappointed to find out how wrong they were. But I still enjoyed the place anyway, the people of Benin are so friendly. Cotonou is a city so if you are after a traditional experience like me, you would not likely get it there. You would have to travel to the traditional parts of Benin. Abomey is one of the ancestral and traditional parts of Benin. It still has a bit of that distinctive past and most importantly, it was the capital of the kingdom of Dahomey. There is so much culture on display in the town of Abomey and there is something new to see every day. Some of the Dahomey people believe in some animals because they have a place in their history. There are some groups whose mythology claims a shared ancestry; a black panther (spirit being) is believed to have transformed into a man that laid with an ancient princess who is their progenitor. They therefore revere the animal. One would observe that the Hollywood Black panther movie was hugely inspired by Dahomey mythology and history. After I had completed my mission there, I made my departure trip taking the Togo route. In Togo, I made an unplanned tour and ended up spending more time than I had decided to spare. In my school days, I remember being taught about the tales of the Notsie King Agorkorli and the Ewe migration. This left images on my mind that played a lot on my imagination. Upon arriving in Lome, I enquired

123

about the distance to this mysterious town called Notsie. When I found out it was not that far, I could not resist the temptation of going. I had already convinced myself it was an important ancient West African society that might prove beneficial to my work. But deep down I knew it was just personal. I have a little confession to make, and it has got to do with my Ewe ancestry on my father's side. This is why the migration story of those days was more than just a story to me, it was history. Well, I did find out about a past indigo tradition here as well as in all other West African countries I visited. I take a good look at the lost kingdom, now, I am facing the remnant of the famous wall. After, I am shown the exit route believed to have been used by those Ewes I descended from. I feel a small bite of emotion at this point, this is where my ancestors had passed.

8

MAJOR SIMILARITIES

I find it pretty interesting to observe similar practises in old fabric-making techniques between different West African ethnic traditions. Different West African cultures have always had different traditions. Spanning from the strip-weaving methods down to dyeing methods used in fabric making, one can see a meeting point. Indigo dyeing, for instance, has been practised by major West African ethnic groups ranging from tribes in Nigeria, Mali, Burkina Faso, Benin, Guinea, Senegal, Ghana, to mention a few. Also, similar methods of dyeing other colours with known plants seem to run through the groups as well. I also used to think mud dyeing was something only peculiar or singular to the Malian culture but it is used by Senufo people of Ivory Coast too for dyeing Korhogo cloth. I was quite surprised to find out it was also practised by the Akan culture in the past for making early Adinkra cloths. This goes to show my earlier assertion that some groups might have had a shared history that has been lost in time. Some might have been part of other kingdoms that declined and led to other waves of migration in groups since African societies are not monolithic. The Ukara cloth in Nigeria is designed with a writing system (ideograms) known as Nsibidi similar to Adinkra in Ghana. These Nsibidi symbols are believed to have been in use before the 15th century. The motifs or symbols of Nsibidi bear meanings as well, which are deep-rooted in Igbo culture. In the past, these symbols were also painted on building walls and used in pottery art. Archaeological findings in the area revealed some old pottery marked with the symbols. This traditional society ran schools as well in the past that educated young ones in the Nsibidi system. Now, this type of schools no longer exist. In appearance the Ukara cloth looks just like the Adire cloth, they are both dyed with traditional indigo dyes. Across African societies, traditional textiles play vital roles. They serve as a special way of transferring culture to the next generation. They are a form of expression and are used to mark different cycles of life. In most of these cultures, the fabric they identify with is made in different forms that serve different purposes. For instance, there are types associated with naming ceremonies, celebrations or festivals, funerals and even in past times, some were associated with war. These were mostly associated with hunting also. This is so because hunting grounds are also considered to be dangerous grounds, making hunters a symbol of bravery. These hunters often double as great warriors too and highly respected in past societies. The hunting (war) garments are sometimes fortified with charms so to give the warrior an upper hand on the field of battle. During some African festival celebrations, one can be in luck to witness some traditionalists display some of this act, performed by a person dressed up in a juju fortified attire and another person firing at them with a firearm. The bullets end up as powder on the garment failing to penetrate the attire and not harming the wearer. Traditional textiles were in past times considered a piece of wealth. In this present day, most still enjoy a certain prestige. Women, in particular, prided themselves in how many pieces of cloth they had. Some may argue it is still the case now. Often at times, the husbands have to make sure they meet that particular desire of their wives. This commodity was valuable dowry in the marriage ceremony as well across African cultures. In the past also these fabrics were considered a medium of exchange, enjoying a special status in the economic system. There were types of these textiles that set one apart from the others, symbolizing status. These types were done by the best craftspeople in the business and were limited in supply. Fabrics that fall under this category are the ones associated with royal households as mentioned earlier. They say some of the best weavers and fabric artists worked solely for such households. In the case of Ashanti, for example, the best craftspeople worked on the king's apparel and some even came from other tribes. There are records of Ashanti people taking textile craftsmen from other kingdoms to their kingdom during past war campaigns. The best artisans of Applique textiles were also in service to the Dahomey monarchs and were paid very well for their services. Royal households employed other expert craftsmen as well such as sculptors, metal and woodworkers. In the present day, some traditional textiles have lost their ancient motifs that carry meanings but in the past, most of the different cultures had their traditional symbols of meaning that were normally incorporated in the fabrics. A tradition that has been passed on to the new tradition of printed wax prints. One would notice that some of these wax prints have been given names and I find myself wondering how the names came about and got informed these names sometimes come from the market circle of women. Most traditional African societies had their system of symbols even before their association with Islam from the 7th century. Some traditions also introduced their symbols (systems) of expression to other tribes. Take the Hausa people for instance who are very popular for their travels across West Africa. I mentioned earlier their travels to Northern Ghana. The indigo fabrics I spoke about which are no longer being produced there used to be made with some patterns and symbols known to be Hausa motifs. This suggests that the Hausas introduced them to their symbols too aside introducing them to their pit method of dyeing. The situation is similar in Cameroon where the

Bamun people there were introduced to these patterns which they used in their work as well. They are believed to have learnt the indigo dyeing process itself from the Hausa people. They are credited for also introducing a species of the indigo plant to that area. The Hausa people are a major ethnic group in West Africa who are mostly Muslims and also said to be the group with the highest number of Muslims in Africa. They helped in spreading the Islamic religion a lot in the region. They were able to spread their religion through their extensive travels and trade to parts of West Africa that were not Islamized at first. Aside from trade, other possible factors contributed to this acculturation with motifs, such as the expansion policy of some kingdoms through war campaigns which resulted in the annexation of other kingdoms and settlements. As we can draw a classical example from the Ashanti-Jaman scenario. We also see the Mali Empire warriors' invasion of Northern Ghana thereby starting dynasties and traditions on this new land which were similar to their homeland, an example is the visible similarity between the architectural features of the Larabanga (Northern Ghana) and Djenne (Mali) mosques mentioned earlier. Symbols are a popular way of African expression, there are believed to be so many of these symbols lost in history and might remain a mystery. Textiles are deep-seated in African culture. It is said that during the colonial era, the traditional textiles industry began to decline because of imported machine-printed textiles which were considered foreign thereby associated with prestige by some. As a result not only did the traditional African textiles suffer but the African arts in general. The arts suffered a decline in this era, going into hibernation because African traditional textiles served as a great medium for these artistic expressions. As they were no longer in fashion, the art could no longer thrive. The two went hand in hand. One could not do without the other. As demand fell, these textiles lost their prestige and value, in turn, becoming cheap commodities at the time. Machine mass productions became the order of the day and many craftspeople in the traditional textiles industry had to change professions because they were no longer making profits. In this present day, only a few numbers of artisans in the rural areas still do traditional textiles but in the past the situation was different. Many people had knowledge in the field or at least in a field of textile production since it was a lucrative business. In present times, there has been a renewed interest of Africans in these same textiles they had turned their back on not so long ago. These textiles have become their symbol of identity and source of pride. Despite the development, these original traditional textiles are not much in supply since they are hand made by a few and also expensive when comparing them to the popular machine-printed textiles.

9

CONTEMPORARY BATIK IN AFRICA

Most countries in West Africa make batiks and the batiks produced in these countries differ from one another in appearance. They all have their distinct look, that notwithstanding, there are still some characteristics that easily make out African batiks in general. It is not clear where resist-dyeing (batik) originated as it has been practised in Egypt, Nigeria, Syria, Senegal and Indonesia among others. Indonesia, most particular Island of Java is the area where resist-dyeing with wax reached much prominence. Even though the actual origin of resist-dyeing (batik) is uncertain, fragments of batiks projected dates back to the first century where it was discovered in Ancient Egypt tombs. Proof of early batik has also been discovered all over the Middle East and Central Africa. Resist-dye is defined by Merriam-Webster dictionary as to print a piece of fabric by repeatedly putting a resist on different parts of the pattern and placing the fabric in successive dye baths. In West Africa, some resist dye methods included the use of cassava paste, rice paste, mud, threads (yarns) and the fabrics later dyed in traditional (natural) dyes. This had

132

been the practise before the popular use of wax by contemporary African artisans. I have learnt from this trip that tree sap was also used as a resist here in the past. In present-day West Africa, most artisans do batiks which involve ready-made (synthetic) dyes, ready-made cloth, Caustic Soda, Hydro-sulphite and wax. These make textiles making less laborious as compared to the past ones, but they still incorporate some earlier elements such as traditional images (symbols) and patterns in selected designs. The Dutch employed Indonesian craftsmen to teach them (Dutch) the craft in the 19th century and not long after this, the Dutch had developed machines for mass production.

It is important to note that African batiks are different from Indonesian batiks. Indonesian batiks are done by a technique of wax-resist dyeing applied to the cloth which involves drawing dots and lines of the resist with a spouted tool called canting or by printing the resist with a copper stamp called cap. With modern African batiks, a technique of resist dyeing is done where on a medium block (mostly foam), various patterns are drawn and subsequently immersed in wax to fix them on cloth. African batik making also involves painting wax artistically on a dyed cloth to create beautiful patterns on fabrics. Most African batiks made in the past involved cassava starch, mud and rice paste instead of wax to resist the dye and later dye in traditional dyes extracted from plants. Other forms included tied and stitched designs (Tie dyes). It also involved the use of simple tools such as spatula, stencils and chicken feathers among others for application of designs and resist to the fabric. Freehand drawing of design was also usually involved in some aspects.

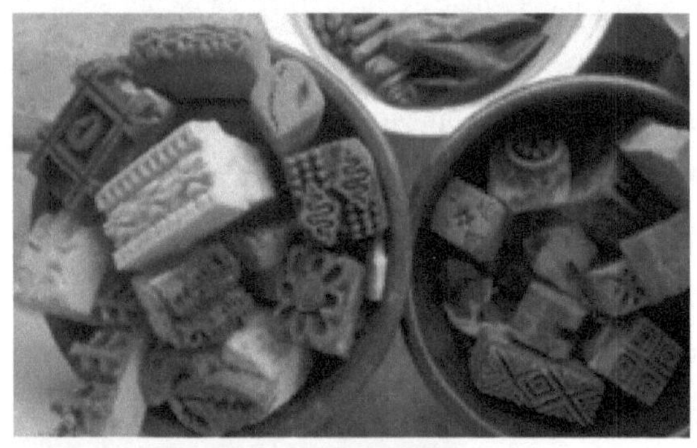

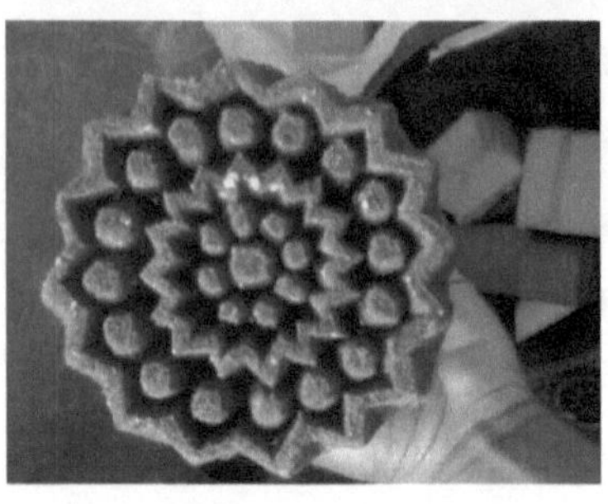

Designs on foam (stamps)

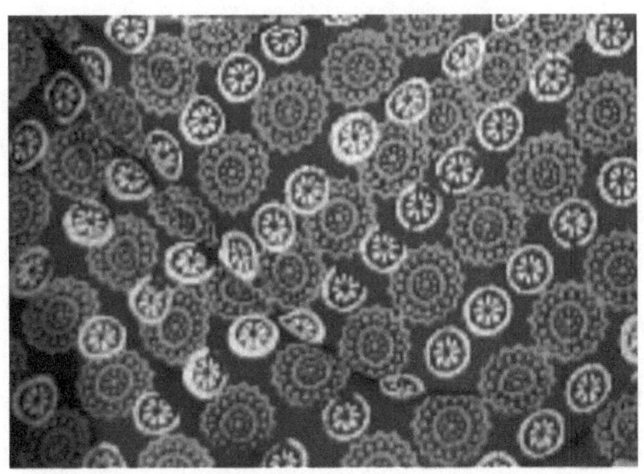

Contemporary Batik textile

How batik started in West Africa is unclear but what is clear is that African artists made their form of art by infusing their culture; adding vibrant and more colour palettes, their patterns, and larger motifs which are characteristics of their old textiles. These became African batiks and survives till date. There is some misinformation in the textile and fashion industry, it is mostly suggested that Dutch traders introduced resist-dyed fabrics (batiks) to Africans in the 19th century. How can this be true when the West Africans have been doing these centuries before? Some surviving West African textiles date as far back as the 9th century and come from the Igbo Ukwu site in Nigeria. Among other examples, we also know of resist-dyed textiles that have been produced in Northern Nigeria from the Kofar Mata dye pits for over 500 years. Even going with the wrong theory of it being introduced doesn't make it any less African, because you can introduce a man to painting but it does not make his paintings yours, it is his intellectual property. That notwithstanding, the art of batik in itself is an ancient practise and no one can say they originated it, you can only own a form of it due to cultural influence. Not to forget, these people (Africans) have a long-standing tradition of making textiles which still bear a strong resemblance with contemporary African batiks. Contemporary batik making in Africa is just a new or simpler way of doing what has always been done in Africa. When the innovation of machine printing was first successful, traditional Asian textiles were imitated using the machine method and introduced to the Asian market. These prints did not do well on the Asian market because the Asians preferred their traditional textiles. Traditional African textiles were also imitated later and produced industrially using the Dutch wax method for the African market. This, however, turned out to be successful. These machine adaptations involved adopting patterns, colours, designs and motifs that are known to be African. The textiles were adapted to the African style and preference of fabrics, all to meet the tastes of this new market after failing in Asia with imitated Indonesian batiks. It is known that the popular Angelina (Dashiki) Print is based on the design of a print on 19th century Ethiopian noblewomen tunic, so as the Nsubura Print is a variation of a drawing of a tie-dye circle motif from 1926. In the sixteenth century as well when cloth currencies were one of the modes of exchange on the West African coast, traditional textiles woven by the Fula people were in high demand. The Portuguese, who were the dominant European force back then did imitations of those African textiles on the Cape Verde Islands targeting the African market. They termed them Barafula.

One thing to note about batik in Africa is that it is mostly dominated by women. It has become more of a women's craft (art) and it is common to go to a workshop and find only women apprentices. The artistic and entrepreneurial spirit of the women cannot be overemphasized. They are the backbone of the textiles industry in Africa dating back from the old tradition to the new. In the past, their work ranged from cotton plucking, cotton spinning (into threads) and also making (designing) the fabrics. They further played key roles in trading these textiles as well. Though in some traditions, aspects of production were dominated by the men, these women still found a way of influencing the final product. Influencing textile designs at the periphery by using pots for indigo dyeing in their kitchens when they were prevented from using the traditional dye pits. These women were also dominant in the old markets wielding much influence in those circles than men. It can be boldly said that this industry in Africa was and still is controlled by women. They remain powerful in the new tradition of fabric making and also in the present-day market circles. In these markets, there are market queens who have significant control over the textiles market and have made fortunes out of the business. A visit to the Grand Marche of Togo and I can still see the influence of women at the helm of market affairs. Same is the case in Ghana's Makola, Lagos market and other markets across Africa. Walking through the streets of Lome market (Grand Marche) and I am reminded of the tales of the 20th century Nana Benz movement. A group of market women who started pennilessly but ended up rich trading textiles. This group of women gained so much influence that they determined which type of fabrics were to be in circulation from the big textiles companies in West Africa and beyond. They became a sort of monopoly, point of entry and distribution for the textile giants through the West African market. These women became so rich amassing properties and were among the few who could afford the Mercedes Benz car in the colonial and early-post colonial era, hence the moniker Nana Benz. They were, and remain a symbol of the industrious African woman. Today, women in Africa still control the textiles market.

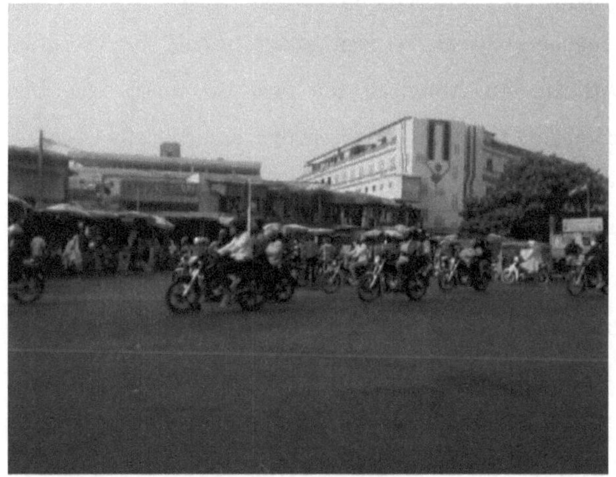

Lome Grand Marche

These women determine market trends, they are gatekeepers and influence what type of fabrics textiles companies churn out.

Many at times write-ups evade and ignore the contribution of African artists in building this brand. The prevailing misinformation about these textiles as mentioned earlier always leads to the suggestion that the popular modern machine-printed African textiles are not originally African. I also got wind of a report recently which was asking whether the machine printed African textiles are justified to be called African. This would be synonymous to asking whether a song sung in African rhythm and African language, by an African artiste should be classified African. An American can own the music recording company but that song remains authentically African. Africans love what they love, wax prints are loved for their African elements, making them African wax prints. Even today if you take an African wax print textile and a traditional African textile, you would not be able to tell the difference between them. You can only tell the difference easily by feeling their texture. The traditional textiles are thicker because of the hand weaving of threads and the wax prints smoother and lighter because of the ready-made (machine) cloth. When the patterns or characteristics of the traditional textiles are used (handmade) on a ready-made cloth then you cannot distinguish at all between them. In that sense, the cloth becomes a contemporary African Batik. That is why all these textiles together make up African textiles. I think most people do not know about the dynamics of the subject because there is not much information too out there, which is why it is easy for people to make some errors. These textile printing machines are primarily for mass productions at a cheaper cost which is simply business. Today some designers and featured inspiration for these textile giants may come from diverse backgrounds, but the blueprint of the line remains African, driven by African preference and style. Even some handmade African batiks are of higher quality than the machine printed African textiles. Some textile giants still borrow inspiration from handmade batik produced every day by African batik artists. One problem facing the small-scale textiles businesses in Africa has mainly got to do with smuggled textiles coming in from China and some other countries. These are mostly complete imitations of the traditional textiles still being produced in the rural areas. They reproduce the exact patterns of the main designs of Kente, Mud cloth, Adinkra, indigo cloths, and even the widely known contemporary batik designs. A cycle seems to be repeating. Because these handmade textiles are more expensive, the average buyers who would have preferred to buy them end up buying the imitations. And they cannot be blamed because most people would not spend much money on buying the textile when they can get just the same look at a far cheaper cost. And these imitations are priced very low which makes me wonder how long the small scale businesses (especially handmade) can keep up production. Anyway, I do not want to sound pessimistic,

African fabrics have been through many trials and transitions and are still here and would be here for a long time (I hope). The art is a form of representation of the African, it is who he is, what he sees and how he speaks. It is in how he sings, how he dances and it is what he loves. It would not have lasted this long if it was not part of his culture and heritage. There is still steady and would always be growing demand for African fabrics. This is a billion-dollar industry and destined to even get bigger. African governments must make meaningful investment and commitment into the sector to reap the benefits.

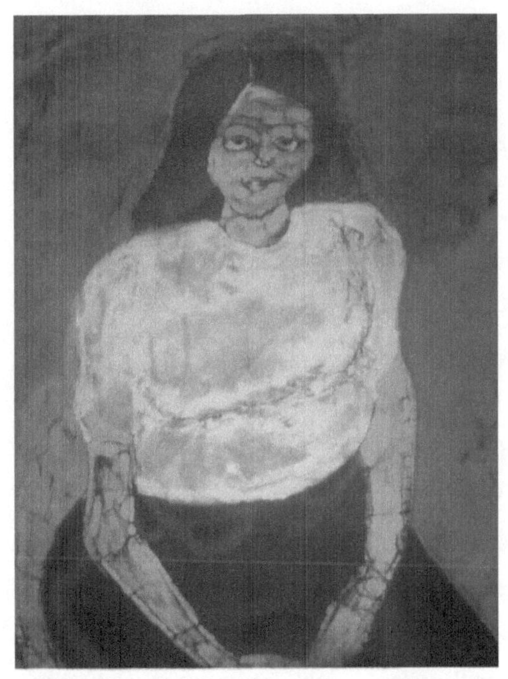

Title: Behold (art in batik)

10

HAUTE COUTURE IN AFRICA

Textile making goes hand in hand with sewing. The beauty of the textile tradition of West Africa is that these textiles do not only end up as cloth worn according to traditional customs. There has been a long-standing tradition of sewers (designers) who were available to transform textiles into suitable clothing (dresses). These sewers made the clothing to meet the tastes of their customers. It was not a trend associated with people of higher status or wealth, it was just a norm. In this present day, this old tradition still survives. It is common to find different categories of people in West Africa with their tailors who take care of their fashion need at an affordable cost. They are measured up and textiles are sewn just how they want it. The designers inform their clients of new trends and give them some options they think might suit them, this is mostly in the case of the women. That is why in West Africa, you would notice people clothed in different textiles and styles during social gatherings such as church services and wedding ceremonies.

In the new tradition of sewing here, you would find the majority of sewers being women. But I have been informed men were also very much involved in sewing in the past. This would explain why I encountered some men in the rural parts during my trip hand sewing the traditional garments there. They only used some simple tool and thread in the sewing process. Their methods of sewing used are traditional, just as the handlooms used in weaving the textiles also. However, this old tradition of sewing is no longer common and you would be lucky as I was to find someone who still does that style of sewing traditional garments. I was quite surprised to find out how old the customized sewing tradition has been in practise although there was a tradition of selling already made garments. This would imply that in some instances people got their customized fabrics made by the textile artisans and got them transformed by the sewers into customized clothing. In modern-day, some West African fashion designers also take inspiration from the old traditional garments, fusing them with modern-day styles and in the end creating something new with roots stemming from the ancient styles. Different ethnic groups had and still have different traditional garments (wear) associated with them. Some surviving styles range from the Boubou style for different genders, the Fugu smock style/garments, traditional hunting garments, traditional army garments, inner garments (shirt styles) among others. Now, among the surviving clothing styles, one can observe a trend where people of other ethnic groups adopt the garment style of other ethnic groups just as the case is with the traditional textiles. The various West African motifs, designs and styles are no longer solely associated with the originating groups but have become general expressions, especially in the urban areas. Sewing and various forms of arts and crafts have been deeply entrenched in the West African cultures and this is probably why in this present day, most people here do not attach that much respect to such professions. Most parents would rather prefer different professions for their children. A child who wants to become a tailor would most likely encounter resistance from some parents because it is considered an ordinary profession which makes sense because they go to their tailors every day to sew fabrics for not much cost to them. Even with the advent of sewing machines in the modern era too, there were still many tailors, leading to some who carried their sewing machines moving from door to door to offer petty home services.

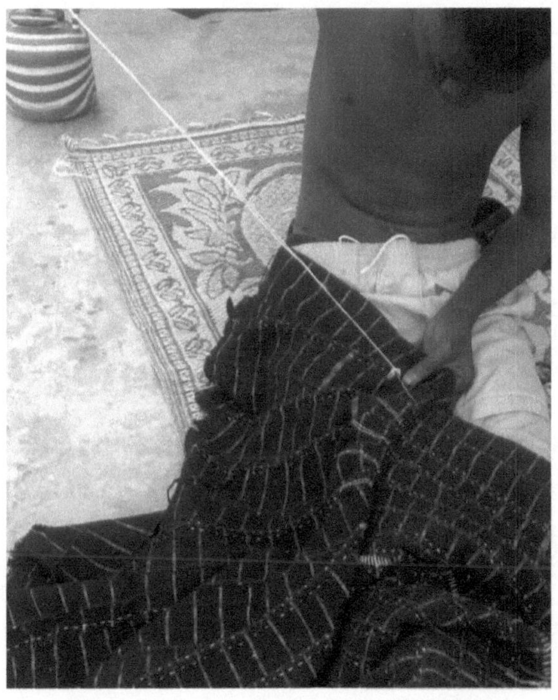

Traditional tailor sewing a traditional garment.

In some West African countries, these individuals were popularly referred to as Adieye. All these played a role in making the profession not so attractive. In some circles, these attitudes are gradually changing, for instance in the cities, this is possible because some fashion designers have gained riches and international fame. This has fed into developing respect for the profession. The growing middle class has also contributed in this regard since more

147

individuals are willing to pay much for their services. Gradually I hope the other facets of the industry would also begin to get their fair share.

Society has to honor their craft and begin to put in the appropriate measures to create a favorable business environment that would sustain these weavers, dyers and artists. They have become custodians of the culture and heritage of different groups of people, which is priceless.

These textiles produced have in a strong way become relics of past African civilizations. They are a visible history that speaks for a people long forgotten. The voice of ancient artists/craftspeople whose work remain relevant in modern societies. It is the end of my journey and I am glad to have experienced these cultures. This was a trip full of beauty. Written out of love. Love, for a continent.

THE END.

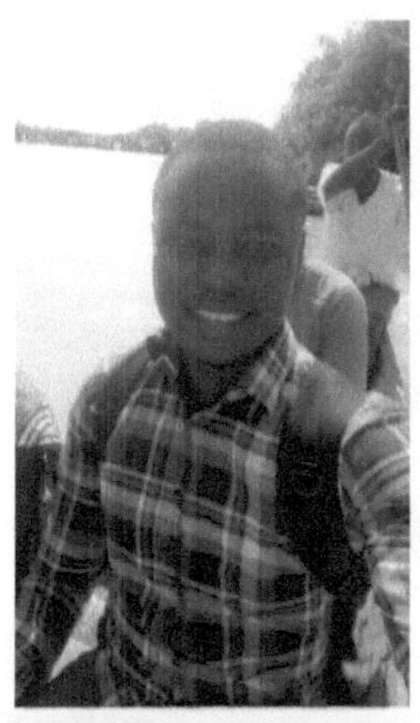

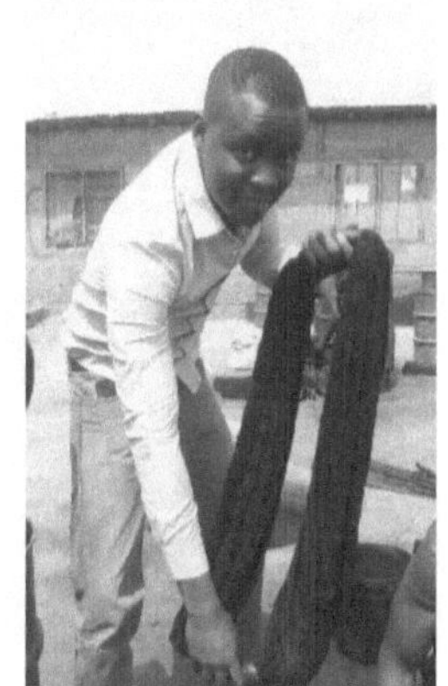

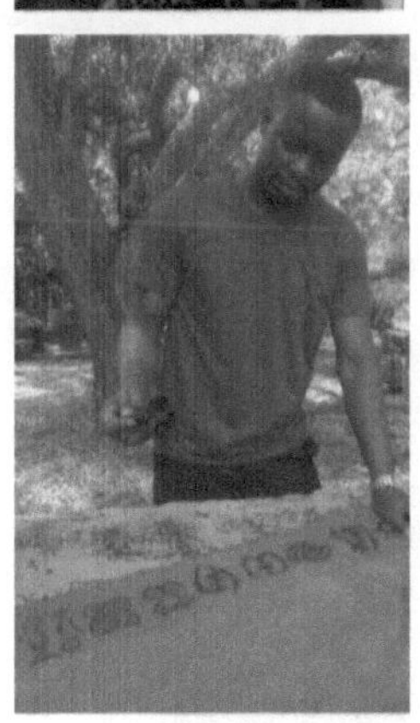

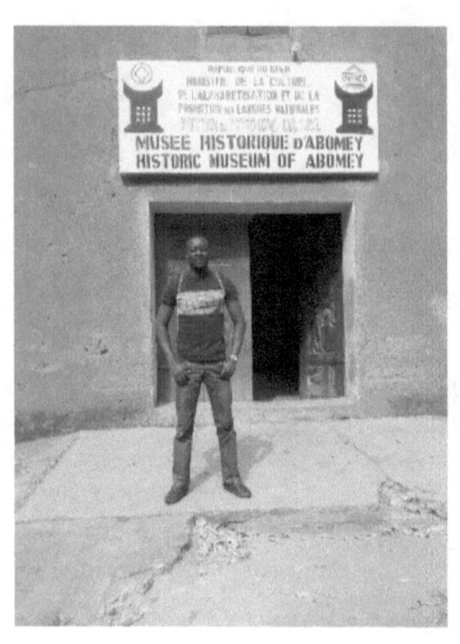
RÉPUBLIQUE DU BÉNIN
MINISTÈRE DE LA CULTURE
DE L'ALPHABÉTISATION ET DE LA
PROMOTION DES LANGUES NATIONALES
MUSÉE HISTORIQUE D'ABOMEY
HISTORIC MUSEUM OF ABOMEY

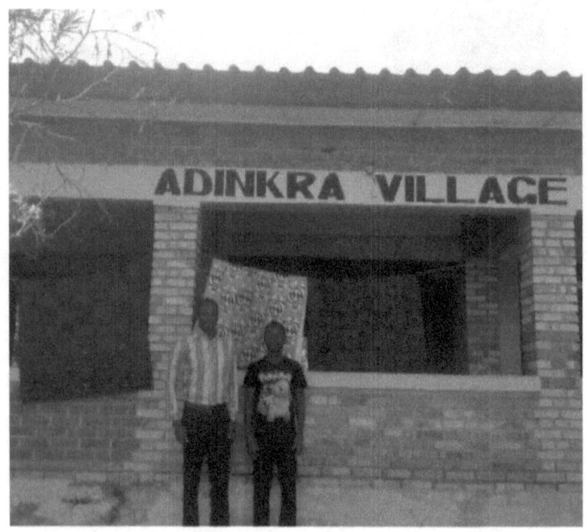
ADINKRA VILLAGE

About The Author

Seyram Agbleze was educated at the Central University College. He is a writer from Ghana whose works explore themes of identity and cultural heritage. He has authored other notable works such as At The Mountain Top, Reflections: Random Thoughts Of A Ghanaian Artist and A Forgotten People; a body of work that highlights some overlooked history of Africa. He is also a leading textile artist in Ghana whose works are inspired by traditional African textiles. On 2022 Black History Month, he was one of the personalities/artists selected by Undocublack Network USA for contributions in uplifting black voices (Lift Every Voice Up Series).He was nominated for the 2024 Africans Rising Awards (Artistic Activist Category). He is a recipient of the Thetis Blacker Award from Temenos Academy, London (patron: King Charles III) and also a fellow of the Merian Institute for Advanced Studies in Africa.

Bibliography

Guan Congress, 6th Edition of the Guan Congress. Short History of the Gonja Kingdom,
Damongo N/R Ghana, 2004.

Claire Polakoff. Into Indigo: African Textiles and Dyeing Techniques: Doubleday Anchor Press, 1980 pp.16-148

Abraham Ekow Asmah and Abas Sherifatu. Deficiencies and Decline of Daboya Local Dyeing Industry in Ghana, KNUST, Vol.14, no.4 (2), 2016

T.E Bowdich. Mission from Cape Coast Castle to Ashantee: With a Statistical Account of that Kingdom, and Geographical notices of other Parts of the Interior of Africa. 1819

Niane, D.T. Africa from the Twelfth to the Sixteenth Century. Paris UNESCO ISBN 9789231017100.   1984

A.A.Y Kyerematen. Panoply of Ghana. Longmans. 1964

4Collins, Robert O., Burns, James M. A History of Sub-saharan Africa. Cambridge University Press. ISBN 9780521867467

Rorbert Sutherland Rattray. Religion and Art in Ashanti. 1927

Atlas of the Human Journey. The Geographic Project. Archived from the original 7th February 2010. Retrieved 10 January 2009

The Batik Guild (1999) the Art of Batik

The Batik Guild. Batik in Africa. Retrieved 29 April 2014

Exploring West African Textile Traditions, Seyram Agbleze , Temenos Academy Review 24.

Agbotadua Kumassah. The Migration Saga of the Anlo-Ewes of Ghana. 2009 Edition ISBN 9988-0-3513-6

Essay on the Superstitions, Customs and Arts common to the Ancient Egyptians, Abyssinians and Ashantee. Thomas Edward Bowditch

Ibn Khaldun among the Ruins. Princeton University Press

.

www.ingramcontent.com/pod-product-compliance
Lightning Source LLC
Chambersburg PA
CBHW051453250726
48655CB00001B/395